The SPEND LESS *Handbook*

365 Tips for a Better Quality of Life While Actually Spending Less

Rebecca Ash

CAPSTONE

First published in 2006 by Harriman House Ltd.

This edition published in 2008 by   Capstone Publishing Ltd. (a Wiley Company)
The Atrium, Southern Gate, Chichester, PO19
8SQ , UK.
www.wileyeurope.com

Email (f

The righ   **Bedfordshire**   been asserted in
accordar
All Righ   **County Council**   d in a retrieval
system o   l, photocopying,
recordin   t, Designs and
Patents   9 39104903   Licensing Agency
Ltd, 90   mission in writing of
the Publ   issions Department,
John W   **Askews**   ussex PO19 8SQ ,
Englanc   71.
Designa   332 . 024 ASH   1 claimed as
tradema   trade names, service
marks, t   The Publisher is not
associat

This pub   nation in regard to
the subject matter covered. It is sold on the understanding that the Publisher is not engaged
in rendering professional services. If professional advice or other expert assistance is required,
the services of a competent professional should be sought.

Other Wiley Editorial Offices

John Wiley & Sons Inc., 111 River Street, Hoboken, NJ 07030, USA

Jossey-Bass, 989 Market Street, San Francisco, CA 94103-1741, USA

Wiley-VCH Verlag GmbH, Boschstr. 12, D-69469 Weinheim, Germany

John Wiley & Sons Australia Ltd, 42 McDougall Street, Milton, Queensland 4064, Australia

John Wiley & Sons (Asia) Pte Ltd, 2 Clementi Loop #02-01, Jin Xing Distripark,
Singapore 129809

John Wiley & Sons Canada Ltd, 22 Worcester Road, Etobicoke, Ontario, Canada M9W 1L1

Wiley also publishes its books in a variety of electronic formats. Some content that appears
in print may not be available in electronic books.

A catalogue record for this book is available from the British Library and the Library of Congress.

Library of Congress Cataloging-in-Publication Data

Ash, Rebecca.
    The spend less handbook : 365 tips for a better quality of life while actually spending less /
by Rebecca Ash.
        p.   cm.
    Rev. ed. of: The new spending less revolution. 2006.
    ISBN 978-1-906-46514-8 (pbk.)
        1. Finance, Personal.   2. Home economics.   I. Ash, Rebecca. New spending less
revolution.   II. Title.
HG179.A84   2008
332.024—dc22

                                                            2008031722

Typeset by Macmillan Publishing Solutions

Printed and bound in TJ International Ltd

Substantial discounts on bulk quantities of Capstone Books are available to corporations,
professional associations and other organizations. For details telephone John Wiley & Sons
on (+44) 1243-770441, fax (+44) 1243 770571 or email corporatedevelopment@wiley.co.uk

CONTENTS

Preface   v

Introduction   viii

Part 1 – The Problem

Or why, despite earning a not inconsiderable amount of cash,
most of it disappears on just paying for the basics

1	Why Does Life Cost So Much?	3
2	The Myth of Low Inflation	11
3	Deranged Consumerism: The Pressure to spend, Spend, SPEND	21
4	Is Money Making us any Happier?	35
5	We're all Going Nowhere	45
6	How Consumerism is Destroying Life	53

Part 2 – The Solution

7 Rules to help you live better, spend less and never let
money ruin your life again

7	Where has this Book got us so Far?	65
8	7 Rules to Help You Live Better and Spend Less	67

CONTENTS

Rule No. 1: Who said you need lots of money anyway?   69

Rule No. 2: Don't let the power of the 'oh but it's only
£20' excuse ruin, bankruptcy or leave you
poor forever   72

Rule No. 3: Rescuing the essential from the clutches
of the irrelevant   75

Rule No. 4: Don't buy new if you can beg, borrow, steal
or go without   77

Rule No. 5: Cultivate an enjoyment of elegant frugality   79

Rule No. 6: Find your own personal financial black
holes and weaknesses   82

Rule No. 7: Always remember that it is about having
more rather than less   85

Part 3 – The Tactics

365 ways to spend less while improving the quality of your life

9	Shopping	89
10	House and Home	111
11	Personal Finances and Savings	131
12	Household Expenses	147
13	Food and Drink	169
14	Unnecessary Expenditure	185
15	Kids, Schools and Universities	191
16	Travel	211
17	Leisure and Pleasure	223
18	Happiness that Money Can't Buy	235
19	Creating More Time in Your Life	243
20	Your 'Job' or Your 'Work'	251
21	Moving Overseas	267

Conclusion   275

About the Author   277

PREFACE

WHO IS THIS BOOK FOR?

This book is for anyone who finds themselves forever wondering where all their money goes.

And why, after the money has gone, they still feel unsatisfied. It is for anyone who feels torn between the elegant simplicity of frugality, and the pure desirability of a brand new Sony laptop or Saab.

WHY READ THIS BOOK?

You are holding this book because there is something you want to change. Perhaps you have a very specific idea of what it is you're after. Perhaps it is just a vague feeling that you want to explore.

This book has two different aims:

1. To help you spend less.
2. To improve the quality of your life.

It also aims to show you how the two are inextricably connected.

But the ways in which spending and quality of life are connected may be different for each and every reader who picks up this book. One person, for example, may find that the tips will help them get out of debt, reduce their living costs and enjoy living more happily within their means. Another may experience a total epiphany that will completely change their life. A third may realise how cost-cutting in certain areas of their life could enable them to take two extra Sholidays a year. A fourth may take away something more emotionally therapeutic or even spiritual.

HOW THE BOOK IS STRUCTURED

So where should you – the reader – start?

Well, the chapters and sections of this book are set out in a logical order and there is a lot of sense in simply reading it through chapter by chapter. But there is no reason why you should not do a certain amount of dipping – particularly in Part 3.

The book is divided into three main sections.

PART 1 THE PROBLEM

We look at the big ideas behind the new spend less revolution. We will take a look at the real truth about where all your money goes – as well as the trends in society that have made spending epidemic. We'll discover why longing for money is the number one cause of unhappiness – and even what the real causes of happiness are.

PART 2 THE SOLUTION

In the second section we'll take a look at the 7 New Spend Less, Live Better Rules that can act as short cuts for our two goals. You can use these rules as little reminders to help keep you on track, as well as reminders about what life should really be about. Here you'll discover tips that will help you turn a £2 cost-cut into a £2,000 saving pot, tips for getting the things you want without having to pay for them and tips for finding true happiness in the life you already have.

PART 3 THE TACTICS

The final section will give you more than three hundred different tips and tactics you can use to both spend less and improve the quality of your life. Pick and choose as you will, or start at the beginning and work your way through. Almost every tip will save you between £5 and £50,000. Many of the tips can make you instantly happier too!

INTRODUCTION

"Always bear this in mind, that very little indeed is necessary for living a happy life."

Marcus Aurelius

The above quotation contains perhaps the most important message from this book that you will take away with you.

This is not to say that this is a book about going without, living the life of an ascetic monk or never succumbing to the desire to buy a Paul Smith shirt or a plasma telly. In fact, this book is about how you can have and enjoy more in your life than you have today while dramatically reducing the financial expenditure it takes to achieve those feelings of beauty, wealth and plenty.

By spending less you really can have more. You can have a beautiful home, wear beautiful clothes and live a full and happy life.

Right now you are probably weighed down, burdened and sapped of life by the endless expenses, purchases and financial worries that obsess, suffocate and dominate our lives. As a nation we enjoy a larger abundance of material goods and wealth than we ever have before. Yet worrying about money is still the single biggest cause of stress or emotional problems in today's world – a condition that affects over a million people in the UK and accounts for one in four visits to a doctor's surgery. And stress is just the start of the damage that a society blinded by monetary considerations and consumerism can do to our souls, our bodies, our hearts and our lives.

The good news, however, is that you can choose to revolt against it and resist the imperative to grow richer and richer, heavier and heavier, yet increasingly hassled and never quite satisfied with your life.

THE PRESSURES OF LIFE

You do *not* have to succumb to the pressure to forever earn more, spend more and pay more for everything. You *can* substitute for the clutter of excessive possessions and expenses, a new and elegant simplicity that allows you to appreciate the power of *less*. And you *can* get back to being the real and authentic you – not a slave to the consumerist society that leaves us always lacking in something, wanting more . . . yet so poor in those things that money just can't buy.

By liberating yourself from the obligations and restrictions that mass consumerism has imposed on your life, you can rediscover the joy of things that really matter, like having soil under your fingernails, the satisfaction of creativity, and an understanding of the real value of the people and truly precious possessions in your life.

What's more, by taking on a new attitude and relationship with money and material possessions, you can go from feeling as if you are leaking money every time you leave the house . . . to feeling immensely wealthy and abundant in cash. You can go from feeling unsure about whether you can make ends meet, to having the pleasure of always having spare money and savings in the bank.

This calls for only a small shift in the way you live, yet it is a small shift that can have an enormous impact on your life.

Many of the tips in this book can help save you the odd £20, £50 or £200 a year. Some can help make you £50,000 richer right away. Others can serve as a complete breakthrough in helping you rethink, reorder or reprioritise your life.

I hope you enjoy this call to a lifestyle revolution.

PART 1

THE PROBLEM

Or why, despite earning a not inconsiderable amount of cash, most of it disappears on just paying for the basics.

1

WHY DOES LIFE COST SO MUCH?

As you're reading this book then I presume it's not because you go out every weekend and spend hundreds or thousands of pounds on designer clothes, luxury items or enjoy an over-extravagant party lifestyle. If it is, then you already know the answer to your problem: stop spending so much money!

So why is it that, despite going without expensive Paul and Joe clothing or even a new pair of shoes for summer, you still manage to get through a bewildering amount of money every month? Why is it that, despite all your efforts to try to spend less, you're still haemorrhaging money at the rate of six or more card payments of £30 or more every week, £50 out of the cash point every few days and a few bills of £100–300 to pay every month? Not to mention the money for the mortgage, the council tax and the loan repayments or the nursery fees.

Well, the first reassurance I can offer you is: *it's not (all) your fault*. As you will discover in the next section, the cost of living is sky-rocketing in spite of the government's attempts to persuade us to the contrary. Today's lifestyle is becoming harder and harder to support, and it really does seem as if there's no way out of it.

> Every part of our lives has been hijacked and robbed of its real
> value by a financial transaction that hurts our purse and emp-
> ties our soul.

As Joe Dominguez and Vicki Robin say in their book 'Your
Money or Your Life':

> *"Over time our relationship with money – earning it,*
> *spending it, investing it, owning it, protecting it,*
> *worrying about it – has taken over the major parts*
> *of our lives."*

From the moment you wake up in the morning till the
moment you go to bed, you are assaulted by a barrage of temp-
tations and (seeming) necessities for spending lump after lump
of your cash. Whether it's the money you spend on your fare to
work or the fuel you put in your car, the £47-worth of groceries
bought on Wednesday that barely last till Friday, the £69
wasted on a meal out with the kids, or the £40 fine you got for
parking on your own street – it often seems that merely keeping yourself alive and sane and getting yourself to work costs
more than you actually earn.

And then, of course, there are the ten thousand and one
other objects of desire that you wish you could own. Because,
yes, we do want an iPod and a plasma TV, a complete new
winter wardrobe and a house full of exquisite furniture.

As you will discover later, the advertising and retail industries are doing more to harm our emotional health and our bank balances than any of us had even begun to imagine. Whether it's large stores luring us in with false bargains, the explosion of new technologies and product advances, or adverts designed to make our lives feel inadequate unless we have what they sell, it's safe to say that reading magazines, watching telly or taking a walk round the shops are all activities designed to empty your purses, your bank balance and, eventually, your soul.

We are unwitting victims of a spend spend spend, more more more, consumer economy that sucks us into a lifestyle where we are constantly spending instead of living; denied the choice to live our lives better.

YOU DON'T HAVE TO LEAD THE SAME IDENTIKIT LIFESTYLE AS ALL YOUR FRIENDS AND NEIGHBOURS

Where do you begin if you want to rebel against this enforced regime of spending and start living your life differently?

Well, one piece of good news for starters is that very few of today's so-called expenses or expenditures are actually necessary.

The spend spend spend imperative is all part of the big lifestyle lie we're told that makes us believe we must get the best-paid job we can, buy the biggest house we can afford, shop at Sainsbury's, eat tiger prawns with lemon grass for our dinner, own a mobile phone with a video camera, eat out at restaurants with our friends, either look like or marry Kate Moss, and work so hard that we never have time to do the things that make us the kind of person we once believed that we wanted to be.

Trying to follow this lifestyle blueprint is literally killing us.

Not only are thousands of us worn down by stress, living in fear of penury or destroying our family life and marriages, we are also trading in our individuality, our connectedness to real life and our right to happiness and a sense of meaning for houses full of endless clutter, frozen ready meals and so much endless consumption that it is making us feel sick.

THE MORE MONEY WE HAVE, THE HARDER WE SPEND AND THE MORE DEBT WE ACCUMULATE

Just think for a minute about the fact that the average person today is said to own 10,000 objects. Yet are we any happier today than we were when the ability to put shoes on our kids' feet was a significant financial expense and achievement in life?

In 2005, the average family put in more hours of work between them than they had ever done before. They earned more money than they ever have done before.

Yet we are far more in debt, more stressed and more likely to say it's hard to afford to live than ever before.

It is not just unnecessary, it is shamingly ludicrous. And, worse still, it is unsustainable. If we go on consuming at the rate we are today, our country will not only be morally bankrupt but physically blighted. Already we are running out of space for landfill. Our children are more likely to recognise the logo for B&Q , Toys R Us or Tesco than they are to know the name for a primrose or a buttercup. Our babies produce millions of tonnes of nappies a year that fill the air with stench and take over 500 years to decompose.

And then, of course, there are the questions of fossil fuels, global warming and worldwide poverty, inequality and corruption. Global warming has become such a soft, almost invisible, phrase these days that we are all able to hop guilt-free into cars, planes and centrally heated houses – oblivious to the fact that by the time small children alive today reach middle age, for example, the Himalayan glaciers will be disappearing, causing droughts that could leave a third of humanity starving.

And what is all this mass consumption and obsessing over money doing to our own individual lives?

Not a lot of good.

MORE AND MORE MONEY IS MAKING US MORE AND MORE MISERABLE

A recent study conducted by ICM Research revealed that, compared to people in the 1950s, the average person on the street today is considerably more glum. Not only do we worry more and laugh a third less, but 45% of people admitted that they wallowed in gloom until lunchtime most days.

In fact, how many people today can honestly stand up and say that they are truly fulfilled and doing what they really want to do in life? How many people can say that the trudge to the office and back, the trawl through the shops on a Saturday, and the slump in front of Friday night telly is a better way of living your life than that enjoyed by people of far less financial means 50 years ago?

So what, we might ask, is the use of rapid technological progress, a massive increase in consumer choice and a huge hike in wealth if it isn't making us any happier? If it isn't filling our lives with joy and passion, and it isn't leaving us with more free time to learn the piano, travel round Cambodia, or sit quietly in the garden and enjoy the quiet splendour of this beautiful world.

And what, I ask again, is the point of working ourselves into the ground in order to pay for the house or the private school that will get our kids the education that will enable them to go to university, to get the job, to do the work, to run round the mill, and to create for themselves an even worse trap of hard work with little real meaning in life to show from it than we are currently in ourselves?

IMAGINE IF YOU HAD YOUR SAME SALARY BUT VIRTUALLY NO EXPENSES

Now let's have a quick look at a completely different scenario.

Imagine if you didn't have to pay any money for housing, and your transport was free. Imagine if you could get free food and if your only other expenses amounted to very little every month – yet you still got the same or at least a similar amount of salary every month.

Imagine, also, that you could wake up in the morning feeling truly alive and full of energy. Imagine if your work was something you felt truly proud of as being creative, fulfilling or good for society. Imagine if your first drink of the morning was a freshly brewed coffee sipped in the garden, instead of an instant coffee in a mug slurped in an over-bright office. Imagine if you could look around the things you own and think: "Wow, I have so much, I am so rich and lucky." Imagine having the time to do the things you really want to do – and getting paid for doing them.

DO YOU REALLY NEED MONEY TO ENJOY LIFE TO THE FULL?

There is a story that I remember reading once about a rich tourist and a local fisherman. It goes something like this:

A rich businessman while on holiday in a foreign land approaches a local fisherman who is relaxing next to his boat watching the waves gently rustle up the shore.

"Why aren't you out there working?" he asks the man.

"Because I have already caught enough fish for the day," the fisherman replies.

"But if you were out there fishing now you could sell all the fish you catch and make extra money," urges the foreign business man. "You could save up the extra money you earn and buy another boat. Keep on working like that and soon you could own a whole fleet of boats and start up a business in international trade."

"And why would I want to do that?" said the fisherman, barely looking up from under the brim of his straw hat.

"So that you could become rich enough like me to be able to sit back and enjoy life."

"But what," replied the fisherman, "do you think I am doing now?"

JOIN THE REVOLUTION

Since the beginning of the rise of affluence and mass consumption in the 1950s, nothing has stopped the march towards ever higher wages, ever greater economic growth and ever more material and luxury goods per person. Today, however, I sense that people are finally beginning to reject this mass spending. Many people want to get off the merry-go-round of mass consumption, overwork and paying too much for everything.

We know that something is seriously wrong with our lives. This book is an attempt to analyse exactly what the problem is, how we can address it, and how we can begin to get more life for our money.

2

THE MYTH OF LOW INFLATION

An acquaintance recently revealed to me that her husband kept all of his unpaid and mostly unopened bills, fines and summons in two leather attaché cases in the boot of his car. She had come across them while searching for a misplaced coat one day and had made the rather brutal discovery that he, and therefore also she, had not paid a single bill in years. Also included among the several hundred letters were handfuls of unpaid parking tickets for which he was now wanted in court – as well as fines for towing away broken-down cars which he had abandoned around the area.

So are we really living in such desperate times? Quite the opposite.

Britain is currently the fifth largest economy in the world. In the last ten years, we are told, inflation has only put prices up by a mere, and historically low, 29%. Our earnings, on the other hand, have gone up by 49%. So in theory, we all should be rolling in cash and feeling happier and richer than ever.

But it just isn't happening.

From 2004 to 2005 alone, the British population increased its borrowings by a massive 12%.

The conclusion would seem to be that, despite us earning more and things costing less, most of us are simply unable to afford the cost of living. So what is going on?

As a nation we spend £110 for every £100 we earn. The average household now has an outstanding debt of £7,713 – excluding mortgages.

THE RISING COST OF HOUSES ISN'T INCLUDED IN INFLATION

Well, the first thing you notice when you look into this inflation figure a little deeper is that it doesn't include the increase in the price of buying your home. Yet if there's one thing I know about the cashflow habits of most of my friends, their outgoings on mortgages are a significant chunk, to say the very least.

In 1971 my mother set her eyes on a house she wanted to buy that cost about £2,500. She had already saved up £900 of that sum from the job she had been working, in a children's clothing shop. The average house price in the UK is now over £200,000 and I can't imagine that anybody these days could rustle up a 36% deposit on a shop worker's salary.

And then, of course, there is the amount we spend on our homes once we've bought them. The likes of Kirstie Allsopp,

Sarah Beeney and Colin McAllister with their ubiquitous property television programmes have made us all believe we can make a fortune out of our own homes as long as we add a conservatory and a loft extension, shell out for a zen water feature in the garden, place Molton Brown toiletries in the bathroom and try to squeeze the contents of *Elle Decor* magazine into our cramped Victorian terrace conversions.

Whatever happened to spending within your means and thinking, you'd come up in the world if you could put a crocheted dolly cover over the loo roll in the outside toilet?

DO YOU EVEN NOTICE HOW MUCH YOU PAY IN TAX EVERY YEAR?

OK, time for a few more facts.

In 1964, Tax Freedom Day (that is the day of the year up until which every penny you earn goes to the government in taxes) was the 23rd April, while today it is the 31st May. In 2005, 36.5% of our average national income went in taxes. Government spending has reached nearly £600,000,000,000 a year (which comes to £10,000 for every man, woman and child). And they now employ over seven million people who earn more than the average person in the private sector.

Now, I wasn't around for enough of the 1960s to remember whether or not we got significantly less return (as in happiness and living standard) out of our taxes, but as far as I'm aware, we had free and very good schooling, cheaper rail travel and hospital beds that didn't collapse at one end when you sat on them (a joy I experienced personally while giving birth to my second child in a London hospital recently).

Still, at least with our economy (apparently) doing so well over the past years, we must be bringing in a good deal more tax from thriving businesses? Not at all, I'm afraid. In fact, while the tax burden for the average working individual is rising by the minute, taxation on big corporations has reached an all-time low under our supposedly socialist current government.

Inland Revenue statistics reveal that the UK income tax take of £48.8 billion for 1989–90 rose to £123.7 billion for 2004–05. During the same period, however, the money brought in from corporations rose only from £21.5 billion to £32.4 billion – not even in line with inflation.

Under Blair and Brown, the percentage that corporations contributed to the tax take in the UK dropped from 11.5% in 1997–98 to just 7.7% in 2003–04.

According to the *Standard*: "More than 65,00 rich individuals live in Britain, but pay little or no tax."

So, while the taxes we hard-working middle classes pay support those out of work at one end of the scale (recent government stats showed that 1 in 12 Scots of working age is classified as too ill or disabled to get a job), at the other end of the scale, we are also supporting the lifestyles of the top 1% of earners. While Richard Branson has received £1.57 billion for Virgin Trains in public subsidies since the government privatised the railways, his company, the Virgin Group, is based in the Caribbean for taxpaying purposes.

As one of my favourite writers in the UK today, Jo Makepeace of SchNEWS.co.uk says, "That's taxpayers' money, for someone who pays hardly any tax, for a service that is crap."

THE COST OF LIVING IN BRITAIN IS AT LEAST 50% HIGHER THAN IN THE US

But surely, some may ask, if our earnings really have increased by 49% in the last ten years, we should still be able to afford a higher standard of living even after we've paid for our housing and tax bills?

Well, no, actually.

Not when we consider what the real cost of living has become in this country. In fact, a recent study by KPMG reveals that when disposable income is compared with the cost of living in different countries, the Spanish and the Portuguese actually come out wealthier than us Brits. The Mercer Human Resource Cost of Living survey revealed Tokyo and London to be the two most expensive cities to live in. Indeed, the price of our food, beverages and tobacco across the country puts us in the top pricing bracket throughout the world, sitting in a group beside Sweden, Finland, Denmark, Switzerland and Iceland.

And, get this: The US Navy pays its service members an extra allowance for living here because it has worked out that the cost of living is higher than in the States to the tune of 64% in London and 56% in High Wycombe or Daws Hill.

From the cost of a can of Coke to the price of your home, we often pay an awful lot more in this country for what often amounts to a lot less.

THOUSANDS OF POUNDS OF EXPENSES THAT WE SIMPLY NEVER USED TO HAVE

There are so many other things that we have to pay for today that people simply didn't have to pay for 20 years ago.

PENSIONS

Take your pension, for example. Twenty years ago, if you worked for a company, it paid money into a pot that would afford you a decent pension on retirement. Today, if you're anything like me, then you pay £30 a month into a personal pension yourself and plan to either get rich in the meantime or live off potatoes grown in your own garden until whatever age it is that modern medicine will keep us going to. Unless you're lucky enough to work for the government, the cost of saving for your pension is rising. The combination of low inflation and low interest rates (not to mention the poor performance of pension fund managers) means that you have to put in a ridiculous amount of money to have any hope of getting much out.

CHILD CARE

Next on my list is child care. With the cost of living as high as it is in Britain today, some 60% of couples with children find that they simply cannot afford to pay the mortgage and put food on the table without both partners going out to work. Yet for so many of these couples, at least 50% of the extra money they earn is eaten up by the rising cost of child care, the money they spend on conveniences because of the busy lives they lead and the 'guilt money' that many parents then lavish on their children.

AND THE REST . . .

And my list goes on and on. It includes the extortionate amount of money you have to pay these days for an electrician, plumber or a little man to rebuild the wall in your front garden; the fact that our rail journeys, according to a survey by the Liberal Democrats in 2003, cost us more than any other country in Europe and nearly twice as much as in France, Finland and Austria; the £600–1,000 you might pay for private health care because your wife heard a (true) rumour about cockroaches in the maternity ward; and the private schools that so many people are now sending their kids to.

THE BIGGEST INFLATION IS IN OUR PERSONAL GREED

And that, I'm afraid, is where the guilt-free reasons for your overspending, over-consuming and over-borrowing end. Because there are two more big factors that contribute to the real hyper-inflation of the cost of living in which you are not entirely let off the hook. These are:

1. *Inflation of the Sheer Number of Things You Can Buy*
2. *The Inflation of Expectations*

INFLATION OF THE SHEER NUMBER OF THINGS YOU CAN BUY

I will cover this first one in more detail in the next chapter, but take, for example, the fact that in 1970 only around one-third of all households in the UK had a telephone. In 1996, only 16% of households had at least one mobile phone; today that figure is 86%. Today, 45% of households have the internet at home.

Or how about the fact that we currently take six times more overseas holidays than in 1971. That in 2004, despite the number of DVDs, Sky subscriptions and game consoles we also consume, we still managed to notch up the second highest number of visits to cinemas for over 30 years. Or the fact that the single publication that has a higher circulation and reaches more homes than any other publication is . . .

. . . *the Ikea catalogue.*

The simple truth is that we spend a hell of a lot more today than we ever have before. And to an extent we can get away with this extravagance by saying there is a hell of a lot more to buy.

But is that really a good enough excuse?

THE INFLATION OF EXPECTATIONS

There was a time when people used to have hopes and dreams for a better future. A hundred years ago a working couple might have dreamt about being able to afford a Bank Holiday trip down to the seaside for the kids. Fifty years ago a house-wife might have dreamt about owning a new fridge or cut corners on the food budget in order to save up for a 'wireless'.

And those were happy, life-enhancing dreams that gave people something positive to live for.

Today, we all believe and expect we should be able to afford all the different luxuries that we see advertised in our magazines. We believe that we too should be able to dress our children in the same designer clothing worn by the likes of the Beckhams, and that we have the right to own our own expensive home, no matter what the cost. We are all party to *The Inflation of Expectations*.

In ten years' time you'll be richer than you are today, right? And that justifies the loans, mortgages and debts you're drowning in today?

Well, like Mr Brown and Mr Blair, all we can hope is that the economy holds up.

3

DERANGED CONSUMERISM: THE PRESSURE TO spend, Spend, SPEND

In 1929, Virginia Woolf wrote that all a woman needs to gain her independence and write a book is a room of her own.

Today, thanks to the march of technology and the *Inflation of the Sheer Number of Things You Can Buy*, I'm afraid the price is much higher and the scene a lot more frenetic.

In fact, all I have to do is spend five minutes flicking through a woman's magazine and I feel filled with lacking, longing and self-loathing if I can't afford the *de rigueur* home beauty treatment from Chanel at £125, a Siemens Porsche Coffee Maker, the same red Hunter wellington boots that Kate Moss wears, a £395 cardigan for casual wear, a pair of this season's 'must-have' sparkly shoes from Miu Miu, and three Indian bedspreads at £350 each to layer on top of each other as a table cloth.

I sit here now picturing dear Virginia having nothing to do all day than stare out of the window. I, on the other hand, barely seem to find the time to get down to the job at hand – let alone gaze at the line of pylons I can see in the distance. Because the truth is that the more we shop, the more we own, the more chores, hassles and complications are created in our lives.

By the time I've sorted out the problem blocking my internet connection, nipped round the shops for a coffee, answered the phone five times, paid bills for my mobile phone and AA membership, sent seven emails and waded through all the junk mail ("Oh, I do like those white Egyptian cotton pyjamas, maybe I'll buy them."), there certainly isn't any time left for quiet contemplation, idle dreaming or even anything resembling careful thinking.

Oh, for just five minutes of peace and tranquillity . . .

THE TRUE COST OF LUNCH

When I started looking into the reasons why we spend so much money, I came across a House of Commons research paper commissioned for the Queen's Golden Jubilee in which life in the early 1950s was compared to what it is like today. Looking down the list of food stuffs I noted the prices for cheddar cheese, beef, margarine, eggs, loose tea, sugar, white sliced bread, potatoes and milk. But nowhere could I find the prices for pre-washed fresh tarragon, jars of sun-dried tomatoes or chicken dopiaza with rice.

So while Virginia could have popped down to the kitchen for a nice cheese butty and a refreshing cup of tea served from a beautiful bone china teapot (milk originating from a real cow and delivered in a satisfying glass bottle collected and reused by the milkman every morning), your 21st century equivalent will need to don her designer sunglasses and Birkenstock sandals, preen herself with factor 30 face cream, anti-ageing foundation and Max Factor Masterpiece mascara and hike to the local shops, returning 40 minutes later with a pair of exfoliating gloves, gel comfort cushions for her stilettos and a new bath toy for the kids she noticed while at the sandwich counter in Boots.

THE REAL REASON WHY LIFE COSTS SO MUCH THESE DAYS

But where (and why?) did all this deranged consumerism and out-of-control proliferation of 'stuff' come from?

Why is it that 50 years ago it was possible to raise a kid from babyhood to adulthood with nothing more than a few towelling nappies, a few metres of good cloth (grey for a boy, gingham for a girl), a slate and a piece of chalk and a hobby horse made out of an old sock tied to a broom handle to keep them entertained in the nursery?

Whereas today you need three different kinds of baby bath (traditional with sponge inset, reclining from six weeks, and rotating action once they can sit), a machine that wraps and seals nappies in individual bags, another machine to heat a baby wipe so it doesn't shock your newborn's bottom, a chair that rocks and plays music, two stages of chairs for the car, a shade for the window, a set of toys on an arch for in-drive entertainment, a buggy that can drive over snow, and a baby monitor with television – before they even get to six months!

The answer isn't difficult.

We spend so much today because there are quite simply so many things these days that one has.

According to a survey by Barclays Insurance, the average person owns CDs worth £1,500 and 8–12 pairs of jeans. Fifteen million new mobile phones are bought in the UK alone each year. The Tesco electric store online lists 130 items from 24 different brand names just in the 'small kitchen appliances' section. And I could probably personally list about £1,000 worth of assorted items that I would love to buy for my tiny back garden.

There are no less than ten different women's clothing stores on an average small town high street.

The simple truth is that there are so many things these days for us to spend our money on – all so cleverly marketed to us that we believe we have to have them. To an extent it becomes the power of advertising versus the power of our wills. But more than that, it is the fact that we haven't thought of saying "no" or "do I really need that?"

BUT WHY EXACTLY ARE WE IN ALL THIS MESS?

Of course, it would be naive to claim that all this wealth and plenty is bad or indeed that conspicuous consumption is anything new.

For the average person in Britain living 150 years ago, life was a never-ending struggle for mere subsistence – only the top sliver of society had any money available for anything more than the most basic necessities of life. The average working-class woman was lucky if she owned her own hairbrush and a pair of copper cooking pots. Women and children often lived on little more than potatoes, bread and margarine. The average man's greatest personal possessions were probably an inherited pocket watch and a couple of starched collars.

But by the beginning of the 20th century things were starting to change – and at a faster rate of change than had ever been known before.

At the very beginning of the 20th century, Henry Ford's Ford Motor Company heralded the start of an era of mass production. His innovation of the assembly line in which individual workers stood at the same place and performed the same task repeatedly meant that more and more things could be made at lower and lower prices.

Then in the 1920s, there was the arrival of plastic. Moving swiftly on from bakelite, which gave us umbrella handles and pipe stems in any shade between light brown and black, we quickly arrived at the proliferation of brightly coloured cups, vases, trays, clocks and Barbie dolls that flooded the markets, homes and eventually landfill sites of the modern Western world.

Today, the cosmetics industry alone is worth billions of pounds, with the faces of Gwyneth Paltrow and Elizabeth Hurley trying to persuade us to part with our hard-earned cash for the latest beauty miracle. *Yet the very first manufactured cosmetic, rose leaf powder, did not arrive until 1891; for centuries women had relied on oatmeal, cucumber, oil and geranium petals from the garden.*

Over the past hundred years an enormous amount of things has become available – thanks to methods of mass production and distribution, marketing and the advance of everything from ceramics to LCD science. In the 1920s, bottles were still made by men blowing down long tubes into molten glass. By the 1960s, pop artists, led by Andy Warhol, wanted to make even art available to the mass of American people. In 2005, the Ikea catalogue promised the population of the world that it really can have everything:

"Jaw-dropping style and new lower prices – our have-it-all approach to affordable design."

EVERYBODY WANTS TO BE WEALTHY

The speed with which the products of mass production infiltrated and moulded peoples' lives in the 20th century was astonishing. A rapidly mushrooming sector of society – the middle classes – was created out of a social and economic model in which more and more things were made and sold by more and more people making more and more things and selling more and more things to each other.

In fact, it is the very fact that everybody wants to be rich these days that means that we have to buy so many things and pay for so many services. Almost everyone is involved in making something or doing something that they want everybody else to buy in order for them to make their fortune. We are on a merry-go-round of production and consumption and it's spinning so fast these days that a lot of people would like to get off.

THE GOVERNMENT IS TO BLAME AS WELL

But please, please, please don't mention it to the politicians, because you might upset their £200-a-head lunch. After all, the standards they've set themselves demand not only that the economy never dare decline or even falter, but that every year we experience even more economic activity and continuing growth in productivity, profit and individual wage-earning capacity.

In fact, it is this obsession with economic growth that has got us in the position we find ourselves today, both as society at large and in our individual lives.

"Having more and newer things each year has become not just something we want but something we need. The idea of more, of ever-increasing wealth, has become the centre of our identity and our security, and we are as caught by it as the addict is by his drugs."

'The Poverty of Affluence', Paul Wachtel

Back at the beginning of the 20th century when this whole mass production, mass consumption thing started to take off, the increased availability of goods and the increased economic wealth it created did do a lot to improve poor peoples' lives.

But how many people could really be said to be poor these days? The government may say that millions of people still live in poverty, but when they define a poor household as one whose income is 60% of the national median, how can we take it seriously when 30 years ago that would have been seen as a fortune?

The truth is that *while the desire to grow richer and buy more things was a good thing at the beginning, it has continued beyond its useful and happiness-increasing scope.* More material goods at the beginning really did improve the quality of peoples' lives, but we have got to the point now that we do not really need any more.

Yet if we are to enable both business and government to meet their targets for year-on-year growth, it is crucial that we never become satisfied with how much we already have but continue to hunger for more.

And fear not, brave shopper, for we are not left to stoke the fires of desire on our own. If modern economics and politics worship growth, then the advertising and retail industries are hell bent on helping them achieve their aim.

THE ADVERTISING INDUSTRY CREATING FALSE NEEDS AND DESIRES

Fifty years ago, industry and commerce were abuzz with the joy of being able to supply people with things they really needed at prices that really did suit their purses. Today, with very few proper needs really unmet, it is the job of these industries to create new needs for us. In fact, they are so successful at what they do that few of us even stop to question the idea that we need a camera on our mobile phone, a TV on the baby monitor or perforations in our roll of cling film.

> *"We see that a newly improved laundry detergent has better chemicals that our older, dull detergent lacks, and that the woman who uses this detergent has a family pleased with*

*their crisp, clean clothes; whereas our family never has a
word to say about their washed clothes, except to complain.
We see that this year's new cars have many improved features
compared with our automobile – although it is only
two years old – and that people who drive these new cars
live in nice neighbourhoods, travel to fun places,
and have sexy, happy spouses."*

'The High Price of Materialism', Tim Kasser

SAVE 50P BUT SPEND £50

You may not be aware of it, but every time you step into a store today you are at the mercy of a whole industry of experts whose job it is to try and make you leave that store having spent as much of your money as possible – preferably on goods that cost a pittance to make but for which you are happy to pay a premium.

Take a look at successful stores like Borders book shops or Tesco supermarkets. You might only pop in for a newspaper or a jar of peanut butter, but you probably won't leave without also picking up a magazine, a video, a turkey baster, a bargain picnic set or a miniature Zen garden.

Think you're clever popping in for that 2-for-1 offer advertised in the window, or the pair of £15 jeans you read about from George at Asda? You won't when you leave the store half an hour later and £70 poorer, and realise that that is exactly why they created the offer in the first place. If they can get you in the store, then they will use every trick in the book to make you spend your money. And believe me there are a lot of them.

THE CUNNING TRICKS THAT MAKE YOU SPEND

According to Richard Hammond in 'Smart Retail' (a book for the retail industry), the 'transition zone' is the area that transfers the customer from the outside into the store. If the zone is too empty, apparently, it could make the customer feel too exposed and reluctant to move into the store. Too cluttered, however, and you could also impede your customers' progress.

Get them inside and you're on to a winner – as long as you have optimum display and presentation factors, a layout that leads people effectively through the store, and you position plenty of extras for them to pick up as they're waiting at the cash desk.

Selfridges, according to Richard Hammond again, is:

"Quite simply the best merchandise store in the world. The store buzzes with the energy and excitement of a Turkish bazaar while at the same time retaining the chic and style of an exclusive Bond Street boutique. The effect is thrilling – the purchase of a pack of Muji pens for £1.50 delivers the same retail therapy effect as does a £150 purchase of an Alexander McQueen shirt."

He has a very good point. Making us feel great as we shop is apparently the most important thing that any shop – or catalogue or advert – can achieve.

ARE CREDIT CARDS THE BIGGEST OF ALL EVILS?

But why *shouldn't* we be able to buy that leather Diesel jacket we so covet, that set of Le Creuset saucepans, that beautiful Apple computer, that Elle MacPherson lingerie set, or whatever designer objects of desire that happen to set your heart on fire and make you feel like you're special? Why shouldn't we have those lovely things that could make us so happy?

Snap out of it, dreamy head.

You can't have it because you can't afford it. No matter how much the advertising industry and the credit card companies in unison try to persuade you that you can.

One credit card mailing I received recently from American Express provided me with a kit for making a purple gift box and told me:

"You can afford to treat yourself more often with the American Express Platinum Credit Card."

In whose world, I ask you, does a typical APR of 14.9% make buying a 'bottle of Chanel nail varnish or a little something from your favourite boutique' an affordable way to pay for 'well-deserved indulgences'?

HOW ARE YOU BEING FOOLED?

Or how about the fact that while we may in our naive wisdom believe that the goods, brands and labels we buy make us cool, we are nothing really other than putty in the hands of an industry that has targeted those brands and goods at our exact age group and sector of society.

Don't believe me?

Take a look at this quote taken from an advert for a $5,695 report on how to sell your products through cool:

"Older consumers still want to be in touch with younger generations and certain products allow them to develop a cool image, fit in with their peer group whilst not compromising their maturity. While younger consumers look to celebrities to define 'cool', young adults and early mid-lifers want products that are unique, stylish and innovative. Individuality, not imitation, is most important for this group."

THE PSYCHOLOGY OF DESIRE

The nature of human desire means that however much we have we will always want more. As soon as one desire is fulfilled, a new and bigger one will take its place. And this is exactly what has allowed *The Inflation of Expectations* to make the greedy, consumption-hungry, material-goods-desiring monsters of us that it has.

The cult of consumption propagated by glossy magazines and television has lured us into the belief that buying lots of lovely things will make us happy, and that without these things not only our lives but also ourselves and our personalities are lacking.

We have lost the ability to realise what we don't need, and have been forced into a culture of want, want, want. Or, as Juliet B. Schor says, this is a whole new kind of consumerism in which 'keeping up with the Joneses' has been replaced with 'keeping up with the Gateses' and everybody wants to be rich, rich, rich. According to Schor:

"Through the boom years of the nineties, as new wealth led to a dramatic upscaling of consumer norms, the pressure intensified. Luxury replaced comfort as the national aspiration, despite its affordability for only a fraction of the population."

No sooner was the housewife able to afford a fridge, than she wanted a washing machine. No sooner were we able to afford cars, than we wanted to own Porsches or SUVs. No sooner were we able to afford new clothes at Reiss instead of Topshop, than we were suddenly window-shopping in Paul Smith, moaning that we couldn't afford that too.

The other day I allowed my three-year-old daughter to watch ITV, because her penny-pinching mum had not forked out for the Freeserve technology that would allow her to watch CBeebies on a Saturday morning as she could through the week. Just five minutes into the viewing and she turned to her father and said, "I want a Barbie."

Everybody today wants more than they can afford. We live in a commerce-obsessed culture in which an advertising industry will continue to sell us more and more until one day we realise that choosing to say "enough" can actually make us feel so much better.

TIME FOR A CHANGE

In our heart of hearts, most of us know that having all those beautiful things we desire will not be the deciding factor that makes or breaks our level of happiness. In fact, many people these days have gone beyond the desire for material goods and now have a stronger yearning for things that money cannot buy.

Enough of all this growth, I say. Enough of all this more, more, more culture. Why can't we just stand still for a little while and breathe in the smell of the day, stop to marvel at our childrens' skin, take the time to plant a tree, write a letter or smile at a kind stranger. In a minute I am going to dig out an old fountain pen, pick up a piece of paper, and go into the garden with a glass of ice-cold milk.

4

IS MONEY MAKING US ANY HAPPIER?

Money, money, money. Spend, spend, spend. It might be driving us all slowly mad, making us hollow and dissatisfied – but governments around the world love it.

The more we spend as a nation, they seem to believe, the better we are doing. Because, when you strip it down to its basics, that's exactly what GDP (Gross Domestic Product), their favourite measure of national achievement and progress, in actual fact measures.

In 1972 the new king of Bhutan introduced GNH (Gross National Happiness) as his country's way of measuring how well its leaders are doing at improving the material, spiritual and cultural lives of their people. While interest in this concept is finally gaining some interest in the Western world, we are unfortunately still stuck with an indicator of our well-being that's based purely and completely on how much money changes hands. Not how happy we are. Not how well we are. Or how much we whistle on the way to work or brim with the delights of life.

"How do you feel today?"

"Great, thank you. I've contributed £1,000 towards GDP this month."

No wonder we all feel so gloomy.

And note that the word 'product' in Gross Domestic Product is itself misleading. As a country that, as of 2004, imports more than it produces, we're going to have to stop pretending that we make things, let alone grow things, nourish things, or allow the beautiful room to flourish.

Those billions of pounds we managed to 'produce' in 2004 is made up of the fact that I sell Guatemalan bananas to you, you sell French bikinis to me, and Tesco sells products created in sweatshops throughout the world to everyone.

Go on, have a look through your cupboards and tell me how many things you've bought or own today that were made by satisfied crafts people in Britain, rather than just sold to you by dissatisfied British shop workers dreaming about how wonderful their lives will be as soon as they've won the lottery.

In fact, while you're at it, open the metaphorical Ikea lacquered fibreboard cupboard of your heart's desire and tell me that a plethora of material wealth and millions of pounds in the bank is the true route to happiness.

Tell me that the greatest source of happiness isn't having a loving partner who you look forward to seeing on their return home every evening. Tell me that happiness isn't the feeling you get when you do something or produce something of which you feel proud and for which you receive praise and recognition. Tell me that the joy you get from being on holiday isn't from being somewhere beautiful and having the time to do nothing. Or that the whole world doesn't just glow more when you've got that real feeling of happiness inside you.

GROSS DOMESTIC CRISIS

The truth is that this obsession that, as a society, we must always have an increasing GDP has an awful lot to answer for. In fact, it is part of what is causing a Gross Domestic Crisis. And it is not just 'gross' as in large, but as in vulgar as well.

Because how is it that amidst all the wealth we enjoy today, all the TVs, DVD players and designer baby bottles that we can buy, we are actually no happier than we were 30 or 50 years ago?

Is it perhaps because saving up for five years and finally getting that bottle green Morris Minor was actually more satisfying than getting that shiny new Peugeot on credit immediately, and which has ended up costing you more in interest alone than the original price on the ticket?

Is it the fact that carefully budgeting how much pork or vegetables you bought for the weekly meals meant that you could treat the kids to an ice cream on a Sunday, or fish and chips all hot in their paper eaten at the end of a pier on August bank holiday?

Or is it, perhaps, the fact that our obsession with money and possessions has led us to take our eye off the things that really matter in life and really can bring us happiness?

IS SPENDING THE NEW RELIGION?

It is no coincidence that almost every religion warns that the pursuit of wealth can bring unhappiness.

In Christianity, Paul, in a letter to Timothy, writes that:

". . . men who set their hearts on being wealthy expose themselves to temptation. They fall into one of the world's traps, and lay themselves open to all sorts of silly and wicked desires, which are quite capable of utterly ruining and destroying their souls. For loving money leads to all kinds of evil, and some men in the struggle to be rich have lost their faith and caused themselves untold agonies of mind."

Timothy 6:9–10

In Islam, the Prophet said:

"This wealth is (like) green and sweet (fruit), and whoever takes it without greed, Allah will bless it for him, but whoever takes it with greed, Allah will not bless it for him, and he will be like the one who eats but is never satisfied. And the upper (giving) hand is better than the lower (taking) hand."

Bukhari

And in Buddhism:

"The true antidote to greed is contentment. If you have a strong sense of contentment, it doesn't matter whether you obtain the object of your desire or not. Either way, you are still content."

Tenzin Gyatso, the 14th Dalai Lama, says:

*"Nor is it a coincidence that we are practically
the first society ever in history that has not been religious."*

In fact, is it any coincidence that the highest and largest buildings in London today are no longer the spires of the churches that inspired love, temperance and humility in the hearts of their flock, but the NatWest Tower and Brent Cross shopping centre, inspiring instead overindulgence, an insatiable hunger for more, and jealousy of the wealth of even the friends you are fond of?

Perhaps we would be better off at the church on a Sunday instead of skulking around the shops, the supermarket or eBay looking for something to do with ourselves?

DOOMED TO BE DISSATISFIED?

In Buddhist philosophy, the greatest cause of unhappiness and dissatisfaction in life comes from the very natural and human habit of desire; a desire that, however much we actually get, is only ever temporarily sated.

When we get what we desire we are not satisfied for long, but go on to desire more. And the glamour magazines, the catalogues and all those shops that seduce us amplify this desire to a level that is making our lives a misery.

I only have to walk past a few shops full of beautiful and desirable things and I can feel that tingle of excitement mixed with the pain of dissatisfaction rising in my chest immediately.

In fact, part of the reason why so many of us feel poor despite earning more than ever before is that there is always so much more we'd like to buy. If only we had more money, we think, then we could buy all those lovely things for our houses and our wardrobes, our hearts and our fingers. But it is this obsession with needing more money that means we are never satisfied.

Only by choosing to be happy with what we already have can we ever hope to enjoy a sense of happiness and contentment in our lives.

"Most of us don't realise we're already beyond the saturation point where more material goods makes us happier."

'Your Money or Your Life',
Joe Dominguez and Vicki Robin

Most of us have lost our connection with the things that used to make us tingle before the windows of Habitat, the adverts on our telly or the designer clothes in our magazines made us slaves to dissatisfaction.

ADVERTISING AS THE DEVIL

In fact, the evil effects of advertising are far more insidious and dangerous to our health, wealth and level of happiness than we might imagine. It is not merely a case of persuading us to buy that expensive pair of trousers or nifty laptop, when slacks from H&M or a secondhand desktop would have done. In fact, it turns out that adland may actually be quite significantly responsible for the hollowness and lack of true meaning at the heart of our society today.

As Steve Andreas and Charles Faulkner point out in their book 'NLP: The New Technology of Achievement', as human beings we are all driven by goals in life. Unfortunately for many these days, so many of the values for which they strive have been given to them by television, magazines and product advertising through what is called the 'seduction of status-based advertising'. We no longer strive to be strong or gallant, noble or bold, but to have our identities and status in life ready created for us by the car we drive, the brand of face cream we buy, or the type of food packaging that attracts us as we walk through the supermarket.

Dr April Lane Benson, editor of a book called 'I Shop, Therefore I Am: Compulsive Buying and the Search for Self', says that:

"Luxury is an illness. If you're buying luxury items because they make you feel more like the person you would like to be or be seen as, that is called the Self-discrepancy Gap. The Aspiration Gap is the distance between what we have and what we want."

According to a University of Michigan study cited by David Niven in 'The 110 Simple Secrets of Happy People':

"Watching TV can triple our hunger for possessions and decrease our personal contentment by 5 percent for every hour watched."

TIME TO RETIRE THE AMERICAN DREAM?

There is, of course, nothing wrong with dreaming. When your life is bad, dreaming of better days can make it more bearable. But can all those well-off people with credit card debts up to their eyeballs honestly claim that they *had* to spend all that money because their level of poverty was making them miserable?

The truth is that very few of us these days can really justify dreaming about better times. The American Dream, as it's called, may have done a lot to improve the lives of people in the US and the whole of the West since the beginning of the 20th century, but it has long ago served its purpose and achieved its goal.

As illustrated in a recent study called 'Zeroing in on the Dark Side of the American Dream', reviewed in *Psychological Science*, where the American Dream does still live on in people, it is doing a lot more harm than good. Throughout the 12,000 people it interviewed, those who said that financial success was important were less happy than those in their income groups who thought it wasn't.

And these findings are nothing new. In the landmark work by Ruut Veenhoven, 'Conditions of Happiness', in which he surveyed and analysed no less than 245 different studies into the factors that affect our happiness and appreciation of life, it was proven beyond any doubt that as long as you're not actually struggling to live, your relative level of income actually has very little effect on your happiness. Your satisfaction with your level of income, on the other hand, does.

In fact, in another famous study it was discovered that *just a year after either winning the lottery or becoming paraplegic, most people returned to the level of happiness they were at before the life-changing event happened.*

SO WHAT DOES MAKE US HAPPIER?

So, if the latest model of mobile phone and a Dior raincoat aren't the route to earthly happiness, then what is?

Well, according to the 245 different studies in 'Conditions of Happiness', the most important things that can really make or break your happiness are: how much contact you have with good friends and company; simple good fun; whether or not you have a satisfying relationship with a partner or spouse; and whether or not you get real job satisfaction from your work.

So giving up that £70,000 a year job to become a park ranger in Snowdonia or a guest house owner in southern Spain could actually make you happier? You'd better believe it.

And what about the deeper psychological needs that we have as complex human beings? According to Reality Therapy and its originator William Glasser, our major psychological needs are for love, a feeling of power or self-worth (through status, recognition or the ability to be respected by others), belonging, freedom (to choose how you live your own life) and fun. So can money, I wonder, buy us any of these things?

Well, an expensive pedicure or hi-tech gadget may make us feel more loveable but then an obsession with one's outward appearance can also be very emotionally destructive.

A high-powered job might make us feel like we're really somebody, but wouldn't you get a better feeling of self-worth from knowing that your work is actually doing good?

Does wearing this year's hippest fashion items make you feel like you belong? Does buying whatever you like make up for having a job you hate? And is that £100 meal out or meander around the shops really the most positive and life-affirming way to have fun?

SO HOW CAN YOU CHANGE YOUR LIFE?

I once met a man who had flown to Mexico with no cash in his pockets and nothing more valuable than the clothes in his rucksack and the miniature bottles of gin and whiskey he had pocketed from the flight. For several months he had an amazing and colourful adventure travelling around the country exchanging mini bottles of Bombay Sapphire for meals, sleeping on café floors, selling his Levis and working in bars by the bright blue sea of a paradise beach resort. He had never, he told me, felt more alive or happy in his life. And he will never again worry about having or not having money.

I am not promising that the rest of this book will give you quite such an adventure. But I do hope it will help you discover how a packet of seeds or a loaf of your own hand-made bread can give you a lot more real happiness than a Gucci watch or a new Porsche.

5

WE'RE ALL GOING NOWHERE

In a previous chapter, we saw how *The Inflation of the Sheer Number of Things You Can Buy* is clearing you out of cash. In this chapter, we are going to look at how *The Inflation of the Sheer Number of Things You Have to Do* (closely related to the former) is clearing you out of time.

Why is it that our lives are so exhausting? Why can we never find time to iron our shirts, catch up with our reading or just stare out of a window?

We rush from chore to chore, from work to the supermarket, from the nursery to the tube station, from the cooking to the cleaning . . . until we fall asleep at the end of the day only to start it all again a mere six and a half hours later if we're lucky.

We have no time for reflection. No time for the really valuable things in life. And God knows we spend more time moaning about our children than we ever spent making them.

But how can it be possible that the more time-saving devices we invent and buy, the less time we seem to have? The faster our methods of communicating, the less time we have to chat?

> We spend more hours watching programmes about nature than we spend enjoying the real thing.

More, more, more. Faster, faster, faster. The acceleration of life is getting to us all.

Ready-made meals, taxis to get us home quicker, dinner from the Chinese takeaway, people to look after our children, a weekly cleaner. We are working forever longer hours to afford the lifestyle we want, yet a great deal of our spending is compensation for the amount we are working – or expenses that enable us to work as much as we do.

And that is only half the life trap that our spend, spend, spend more, more, more culture is tricking us into.

LIFE WAS NEVER EASIER, JUST A LOT MORE SIMPLE

Why are our lives so hectic?

Because there's so much *stuff* in them. Every aspect of our lives these days is becoming more and more complicated, more and more hassled. And the thousands of pounds we spend to make our lives better end up making it harder.

The truth is that the more 'stuff' we have, the more complicated our lives become. Our already-busy schedules are weighed down by the things we have bought, the things we need to buy and the things we want to buy as soon as we've worked hard enough to afford them. Even our 'inner dialogues' are saturated by the objects, the material possessions, the financial transactions, the financial concerns and the non-stop shopping and spending requirements that are literally littering and depressing our lives.

> *"Which of my 27 shirts or T-shirts shall I put on this morning?"*

> *"Where do I buy a cable so I can download my videos onto my computer?"*

> *"Who do I need to ring about my broken washing machine?"*

> *"Must dig out old ethnic jewellery to keep up with this year's fashion . . ."*

We work so hard so that we can have money to spend, but then the money we spend still makes us work even harder.

Dealing with junk mail. Setting the burglar alarm. Sorting out a mortgage. Wading through over-full drawers and cupboards whose contents we've lost count of. Trying to find somewhere to store the dozens of new items of children's clothing their grandparents have bought for them. Even when we're not working, there are a thousand and one chores to occupy our lives and millions of bright images and hectic-making technology that flick through our consciousness and turn our lives into a living nightmare.

As John de Graaf, author of 'Affluenza' and US co-ordinator of the 'Take Back Your Time' campaign (www.timeday.org), says:

> *"We spend more time shopping, struggling through*
> *the aisles of over-choice, or trying to decide between*
> *dozens of nearly identical telephone plans, or erasing*
> *spam on our computers, or commuting through*
> *gridlock, or navigating through voicemail hell.*
> *Unpaid overtime, all of it."*

EXPERIENCES FLY BY ALMOST UNNOTICED AS WE MOVE ON TO THE NEXT

Another cause of our thin but hectic pace of life is our Western obsession with trying to make the most out of every minute. Of not letting a minute pass without having to cram some kind of useful activity into it. And if desire and greed and *The Inflation of Expectations* are to blame for our over-consumption of material goods, then they are also to blame for our feeling that we never have enough time as well.

We not only have a constant 'I want, I want, I want' about things we want to buy. Our longing also kicks in on things we want to do. We are all so desperate to fit so much into our lives that we rarely take enough time to properly enjoy the things we actually do. The overall result is a general feeling of dissatisfaction and discontent and a vague idea that something might be wrong here.

"Tempted and titillated at every turn, we seek to cram in as much consumption and as many experiences as possible. As well as glittering careers, we want to take art courses, work out at the gym, read the newspaper and every book on the bestseller list, eat out with friends, go clubbing, play sports, watch hours of television, spend time with the family, buy all the newest fashions and gadgets, go to the cinema, enjoy intimacy and great sex with our partners, holiday in far-flung locations and maybe even do some meaningful volunteer work. The result is a gnawing disconnect between what we want from life and what we can realistically have, which feeds the sense that there is never enough time."

'In Praise of Slow', Carl Honore

Now, having lost the ability to enjoy the simple things in life or even just do nothing, we have reached such a hectic pace of being that we actually feel funny when everything stops spinning. "What shall I do with this spare three minutes while the kettle is boiling?"

Like children, we want instant pleasures, instant gratification, bright lights, knobs and buttons. And as all parents know, this level of stimulation is exhausting and unsustainable.

Most of the things we do today are an act of consumption, and consumption by its nature is never really sated.

"An insatiable thirst for the new, for the next, for the neural numbing of life lived as one long shopping spree… 'life in the fast lane' is the aspiration of countless millions, regardless of the career crashes and life-wrecks that litter that particular lane."

Jonathan Porritt in *Resurgence* magazine

SO WHERE IS ALL THIS HASTE TAKING US?

In the want, want, want culture of the 21st century and we want it both ways. We want to be rich enough not to have to work, but we need to work our lives away in order to try and achieve that.

So we get well-paid jobs in order to afford the life we want, but watch the rest of our lives disappear in a blur of over-activity. And the sad thing is that all the extra money we earn goes on paying £6,000 a year on nursery fees, £3,000 on the trains into work, £3,000 on expensive clothes and holidays and treats for the kids £2,000 a month on the expensive house near the commuter line, purely because we can afford it.

And many people don't even realise that they are taking their life too fast.

Wouldn't we have been better off working three hours a day nearby, and spending the rest of the day pottering about the garden and having time to watch the sun set?

The odd truth is that having too much money can actually ruin the quality of your life. Having too much and doing too much can rob us of the pleasure of things that take more time than we are able or willing to give them. The pleasure of making bread by hand. The pleasure of really taking time to chop vegetables, stew stock and cook a simple but pleasant meal. The pleasure of sitting down and writing a letter or putting our thoughts down into a diary.

It seems that we are out of step with the real life, with the proper pace of life. Moving too fast to enjoy our lives or the world around us properly.

But where is it that we are trying to get to at such speed?

To the end of the day? To the end of our lives? To that magical day when we'll have nothing else to do but sit on a beach and watch the sun go down, or dedicate a whole month to reading the complete works of Shakespeare, *War and Peace* or the Bible?

SO WHAT IS THE SOLUTION?

Getting off the merry-go-round of activity and consumption can be easier than you think. Remember that the less you spend, the less you will have to do. Make a conscious effort to take more time doing the important and meaningful things in your life. Do them in a manner that is calm and unhurried, really aware and slow and mindful.

Most of us would probably agree with the saying: *Less is more*. So shouldn't we all put more effort into finding out exactly what this 'less' might mean?

○ 'Less' is taking 30 minutes of an evening to just sit in a quiet room and breathe in the cool silence, or taking the time to think back over the last week and realise all the wonder it has contained.

○ 'Less' is forgoing the shopping trip into town and staying at home to start that meaningful thing you so long to do as soon as you have the time.

○ 'Less' is taking the kids on a walk in the countryside and spotting a woodpecker on a tree.

I have a vivid memory of my grandfather bringing in potatoes from the garden, stopping on the way to chat to the neighbour over the fence as the late August sun was beginning to set. I don't know how much longer it took him to plant and dig up potatoes over the summer compared to the time I put in buying my spuds from the shops. I do know that there was a lot more pleasure and satisfaction to be had from the crunch of the garden fork into the quiet warm soil than there ever is from a mad dash through the supermarket on the way home from work.

6

HOW CONSUMERISM IS DESTROYING LIFE

Here's an interesting fact for you: If Star Wars was a country, its revenue of £20 billion would make it the 70th richest country in the world – ahead of Bulgaria, Cyprus and Iceland in the World Bank's ranking of countries' GDPs.

Now, if you picture an image of Cyprus or Iceland in your mind's eye, what do you see and how does it make you feel?

A solitary donkey wandering down a hot sunny path? Warm, relaxed and happy? Stunning glacial landscape? Alive and invigorated?

Now picture £20 billion worth of Darth Vader masks, Chewbacker alarm clocks and Star Wars candy sweet wrappers.

How do you feel now?

Hassled and scratchy? Somehow dirtied? Uncomfortable and perhaps even guilty?

It's no wonder then that most of us choose places of natural beauty to escape to for our holidays. An escape, perhaps, from all the mass of traffic, shopping and consumer goods that weigh down our lives.

But, as ever in our society, we want to have our cake and eat it. We expect to be able to fill our houses with mountains of crap produced in factories and sweatshops throughout Asia, yet also escape there to the unspoilt beaches for our indulgent Western honeymoons (where, having spent the last three months consuming cans of Slimfast and Dr Atkins diet chocolate bars, we gorge ourselves on the eat-as-much-as-you-like buffets).

Those beaches, however, are not going to stay unspoilt for long, nor, I'm afraid, are most of those svelte wedding-day figures.

You know the arguments, you've seen the films and the documentaries. Then how is it that most of us make little more effort to protect the planet than buy the odd organic product and occasionally pick up the recycled black bin liners when we're feeling particularly flush one month in Sainsbury's? Why is there such a massive discrepancy between what we know about the threat to the environment and the way we live our lives?

WHAT A LOAD OF RUBBISH

Let us start, perhaps, with the fact that every two hours the British throw away enough rubbish to fill the Albert Hall. Our tiny but beautiful country simply cannot just swallow up this amount of rubbish, and we are fast running out of landfill space to dispose of the 430 million tons of waste that we produce each year.

We British, apparently, get through 460,000 tons of plastic bottles alone and 8 billion carrier bags a year. Yet I will always remember the sight of small children at an Ethiopian market-place selling old and dirty used carrier bags as a sought-after commodity.

What is 'rubbish' if it is not more stuff than we need? And when a country produces as much rubbish as this, then surely it is a sign of oversupply and overconsumption. 'Dustbins', note, got their name from the fact that the main thing that was put into them was dust from the grate of the fire. In olden days, all food rubbish went into the compost to help grow more vegetables in the garden. Scraps were made into new things and recycled. Packaging amounted to the odd paper bag, and 'disposable' was a negative word that meant something that one could easily do without.

And our weekly rubbish is just the start of it.

Judging by current turnover rates, it is estimated that each of us in our lifetimes will get through 12 washing machines, 10 fridges, eight cookers, three dishwashers, 95 small electronic household appliances, 35 pieces of IT equipment and 55 pieces of recreational equipment; the majority of which will end up in landfill.

And then, of course, there are all the processes of production, storage and supply that got all that stuff into our homes in the first place. Every over-packaged ready-made meal, every £3.99 picnic set or hand-held plastic fan that you mindlessly pick up as you stroll round the shops or the supermarket means another factory to pollute our rivers, another warehouse to replace a chunk of countryside, another out-of-town supermarket to blight the landscape. And another Self Storage warehouse we can use as overflow for our houses when the mountains of excess stuff that we consume and accumulate become more than our homes can handle.

Every new thing that we manufacture and consume means more acid rain, more pollution – and a little less space for mouse-eared bats, Essex emerald moths, Ivell's sea anemones, Norfolk Damselfly, burbot fish, horned dung beetles or summer lady's tresses: just some of the hundreds of species that have been squeezed out of existence in the last 50 years in Britain alone (source: www.englishnature.org.uk).

POLLUTION COULD EVEN BE MAKING YOU SICK OR SLOWLY KILLING YOU

This affects all of us. Over half of the homes in England and Wales are thought to be exposed to noise levels exceeding the World Health Organisation's recommended daytime level of 55 decibels.

A study by the European Commission recently calculated that air pollution reduces life expectancy by an average of almost nine months across the European Union, and is believed to result in more than 32,000 premature deaths in the UK each year alone. Asthma, eczema and even heart disease are now all linked to pollution and are all on the rise. Another study by George Knox at the University of Birmingham suggests that most cases of childhood cancer are probably caused by air pollution inhaled by a mother during pregnancy.

IT IS THE WEALTHY FEW WHO ARE OVER-CONSUMING THE WORLD

Right now, the US, with only 6% of the world's population, consumes 30% of its resources. And, according to the *New Internationalist* (September 1992):

"Each Briton uses on average around twenty times as many resources as each person in the Third World."

If the remaining 90% or so of the world's population were to consume on this level (and that is what they're being trained to aspire to by both international governments and retail and advertising conglomerates) our planet would simply not be able to support it.

"If every adult or family in the world owned a car, these emission levels would be beyond any technological solution."

www.enough.org.uk

"Juggernauts delivering enough telephones for the Chinese population to reach US levels of phone ownership would stretch nose-to-tail for 247 miles."

www.enough.org.uk

But what is perhaps most shocking and gut-wrenching still is the unbelievable amount of fossil-fuel consumption that goes into producing every bit of food that we put into our bodies.

"Since the 1960s it has been true to say that food equals oil. In 1944 the average US farm produced 2.3 thousand calories of food for every calorie of fossil fuel inputs. In 1974 the ratio became 1:1, in our own time there are no reliable statistics but it may be as much as 1000 calories of oil-energy to produce as each calorie of food energy, given that nitrogen fertilisers are made from natural gas (itself a by-product of oil); pesticides

and insecticides are synthesised from oil, tractors and combines run on diesel, and then there's plastic packaging, refrigeration and four-figure food miles. As Heinberg says, 'in terms of energy return on energy invested, industrial agriculture is the least efficient food distribution system the world has ever known.' Hoe and scythe classes anyone?"

www.schnews.org.uk

The amount of resources on this planet is finite. We are quite literally consuming our precious planet until there will come a day when there is nothing of any worth left of it. We're not just biting the hand that feeds us – we're eating it alive.

'GLOBAL WARMING' OR 'ENVIRONMENTAL COLLAPSE'?

So how about global warming?

How come that this terrifying concept does very little to change the way we act? Perhaps it is too mild a term? Perhaps if we replaced it with 'global environmental collapse' it would begin to make you shudder – because that is exactly what most scientists these days are unanimously predicting.

"If current predictions of population growth prove accurate and patterns of human activity on the planet remain unchanged, science and technology may not be able to either prevent irreversible degradation of the environment, or continued poverty for much of the world."

The Royal Society and The US Academy of Sciences

Okay, so you already know that that the earth is warming up due to a build up of CO_2 in the atmosphere created by the vast amounts of fossil fuels we consume as energy. You know that this has been causing hurricanes, flooding, ice cap melting and untold environmental mayhem around the planet. That crocuses that used to flower in March are now appearing as early as January. That coral reefs – containing a quarter of all known sea fish – are likely to completely disappear in the very near future. That 20,000 people in Europe died from the heatwave of 2003. That, globally, the 10 warmest years on record have occurred since 1990. That spruce bark beetles have killed 2.3 million acres of trees in Alaska because warmer winters have caused an explosion in their population.

But what if I told you that the whole world as we know it could be changed beyond recognition within just a decade?

"Based on an extensive review of all the relevant scientific literature, many leading climate scientists now conclude that we have a decade or two before we cross a crucial 'tipping point' where average global surface temperature rises to more than two degrees centigrade above its pre-industrial level.

Just as the onset of a tumour is not instantaneously fatal but sets the course for what is to come, exceeding the planet's 'tipping point' sets us on course for abrupt, accelerated or runaway climate change. This could entail massive agricultural losses, widespread economic collapse, international water shortages, huge rises in sea levels, a shutdown of the Gulf Stream, and refugee problems on a scale not yet experienced – global catastrophe that would continue for tens of thousands of years."

Paul Allen, Development Director at the Centre for Alternative Technology, in *Resurgence* magazine

The answer?

WE LIVE IN A THING-ORIENTED SOCIETY

Thirty years ago, Martin Luther King warned that:

"We must rapidly begin the shift from a thing-oriented society to a person-oriented society. When machines and computers, profit motives and property rights are considered more important than people, the giant triplets of racism, militarism and economic exploitation are incapable of being conquered. A nation can flounder as readily in the face of moral and spiritual bankruptcy as it can through financial bankruptcy."

A hundred years ago, William Morris and the Arts and Crafts Movement warned against the rise of soulless mass-produced items and the 'terrible and inhuman toil' that their production necessitated and inflicted upon the lives of millions.

Five hundred years ago, Christopher Columbus noted in astonishment in his diaries how the native people of America held no personal property, but everybody in the society shared everything that was owned. If you asked a person to give you anything that seemed to be theirs, he observed, they invited you to share it with love in their hearts.

This book is not advocating that we give up all material possessions and live in teepees together. It is merely suggesting that if we all become just slightly less 'thing-oriented', if we all put a little more care and thought into the impact of things that we buy, our own lives may not only be a lot better for it, but we may also save the planet for our children and their grandchildren.

PART 2

THE SOLUTION

7 Rules to help you live better, spend less and
never let money ruin your life again

7

WHERE HAS THIS BOOK GOT US SO FAR?

Well, so far we've managed to excuse ourselves pretty well. We've managed to blame inflation for our inability to keep hold of our cash. We've blamed the advertising and retail industries for our inability to rein in our runaway lusting for endless material goods. But surely, at some point, we have to start taking responsibility for our actions. Because (at least for the foreseeable future) neither industry nor government are going to volunteer to do it for us.

So why is it that when we arrange to meet up with friends, we arrange to do it over an expensive lunch? Why do we seem unable to even feed and clothe our family without spending more than we really earn? Why are there so *many* things that we seem to constantly need to buy? Why does simply getting a decent education for our children mean that we have to work so hard to pay for it that we never get to see them? And why do we spend so much time fretting about money, when having to make do on less or even losing your home would probably not make a huge difference to your long-term happiness?

Because we haven't thought of living any differently.

Because we have all slipped into habits where we no longer question the need to spend money.

Because as soon as we earn more money we will very quickly find ways of spending it. Spending more and more creeps up on us over the years. When we were 18, £400 a month was somehow enough to pay for a room to sleep in, keep us in pasta, beans and tins of tomatoes to eat, with enough left over for beer, fags and parties to make these some of the best and most carefree years of our lives.

But then we get older (and I know, surely that in itself should earn us the right to a five-bedroom house and a walk-in wardrobe full of fine suits and summer linen). And the more money we earn, the more we find new ways of spending it. In fact, it's not that we eat out more, have more fun or dress any better than we used to. We just increase the ticket price of everything we buy. We spend £2,000 a month on a mortgage instead of £700 on rent; £120 on modern European food instead of £15.00 on a vindaloo, poppadoms and two pints of lager; £60 on a new top instead of £13 at a vintage clothes shop in Covent Garden.

8

7 RULES TO HELP YOU LIVE BETTER AND SPEND LESS

PUTTING MORE VALUE INTO EVERY FIVER

The third part of this book will give you 365 ways of spending less on everything you buy, own or do. But it's not just about saving £100 on your council tax or £70 on your mobile. It's about making a subtle change to the way in which we live. It's about thinking differently. And understanding what's really at play here.

Here are some questions that we're about to start answering:

○ How can we spend less and learn to be better with money?
○ How can we simplify and unclutter our lives and enjoy less instead of more?
○ How can we enjoy more quality – in both the things and objects we own, and in every minute of every day that we have left to live on this beautiful planet?
○ How can we work less hard yet feel that we have a plentiful amount to live on?

○ How can we make the way we spend our money more meaningful rather than shameful?
○ How can we reduce the hold that money has over our lives and reverse the tables so we actually get *more living*– and feel so much richer without ever going without?

The following 7 Rules are not given here as some strict regime that you must adhere to. They are here to trip you painlessly and effortlessly into a slightly different groove of spending and attitude towards wealth and money that will flick a switch in your life.

Simply read through and let the ideas work their magic.

RULE NO. 1:
WHO SAID YOU NEED LOTS OF MONEY ANYWAY?

As Marcus Aurelius was already telling us back in the 2nd century AD, it's always worth bearing in mind that little is really necessary for living a happy life. Study after study has proven beyond any doubt that more money does not lead to more happiness. And in fact, most of the best things in life actually are free.

Of course I'm not saying that I wouldn't be over the moon if somebody rang me up and told me I'd just won £10,000 worth of shopping vouchers for Selfridges. All I'm saying is that it's always worth giving yourself a regular reminder that having more money isn't all it's cracked up to be.

So what if you could afford that £900 outfit, that £30,000 car, or that really wonderful house you dream about? Imagine how upset you would be if you fell over in the snow and ripped the knee of the trousers, the car got crunched in a car park or you found that your wonderful new house had a rat-infested pond or a previous owner who'd topped himself.

The truth is that simply understanding a bit about basic human money psychology can go a long way towards making you feel almost quite smug about where you are financially.

○ Never forget that desire is a major cause of unhappiness and that having more money and more things won't make you happier. Remember that by training yourself to actually want or desire less you will reduce the amount of unrequited longing and dissatisfaction that can really make you feel miserable. Instead of walking through the shops filled with the unhappy sensation of "I wish I had everything", you can actually learn to switch off desire and say "I'm happy with what I've got".

○ Always remember that happiness has to come from contentment within. It's so easy these days to get caught up in the national epidemic that turns us all into zombies on a one-track journey towards 'more money'. Put your energy into making your life better, not just buying more.

○ Bear in mind too that you are probably already in the top 5% of the richest people in the world. OK, so there are that 1% at the very top who can afford the £9 million houses and private planes. But is there really any chance – or even any point – in you being able to close up the gap?

> Make the decision today to take a different journey – following the route to more happiness rather than simply just more money.

○ Make a list – here and now – of activities that would fill your life with more happiness and meaning. Whether it's going back to university or just taking a walk in the countryside; having a job you really love or more time to spend with the children; taking up archery or learning to become a potter. Always remember that life will soon be over and that the really meaningful things in life are the ones that are free.

○ Don't let worries about money terrorise your life either. Live within your means that you have today – not some dream income you believe you'll be earning in the future. Think about what would happen if you lost every penny and thing you own and were left with nothing and had to start from scratch again. Would that really be so terrible?

"A simpler lifestyle leaves space for one's spiritual renewal."

'Timeless Simplicity', John Lane

RULE NO. 2:
DON'T LET THE POWER OF THE 'OH BUT IT'S ONLY £20' EXCUSE RUIN, BANKRUPTCY OR LEAVE YOU POOR FOREVER

How many times in the last year do you think you've let money flow out of your bank account by saying the words "Oh, but it's only £2" (or £5, £25 or £2,000)? Whether it's that Disney magazine your child never really needed, £7 wine instead of £5 (every night), or getting the removal company to pack for you when you moved?

The truth is that that £2, £20 and £200 here and there can easily add up to £300 a month or £5,000 a year before you know it.

A friend of mine recently worked out that he'd been spending over £1,500 a year on Starbucks coffee. Each coffee was 'only £2.50'. But, one coffee, three times a day, five days a week, 45 weeks of the year adds up to £1,687.

I can reveal to you a secret of the junk mail industry: If you mail people an offer for a subscription at £14.50 a quarter, up to five times more people will subscribe than if you offer it at £58 a year!

So you see, it's those small amounts that all add up to rob you of your money.

○ Next time you hear yourself think "oh, but it's only…" catch yourself in the act and ask yourself if that expense is really necessary. Will it really add that much extra quality or enjoyment to your life? Only if the answer is a resounding "yes", should you go ahead with the purchase. You'll be amazed what a great feeling you can get from saying "no".

○ Spend an hour one night going through your list of standing orders, direct debits and bank statements. Are there any of those regular payments that you could now cancel? Magazine subscriptions, for example, are a common culprit. Also go through every debit card or cheque transaction and ask yourself whether you could have done without that particular purchase.

○ Spend five minutes every night for a week (and preferably two) writing down every last little thing that you spent your money on. Think about each purchase one by one – and don't forget to work out how much they would cost you over the year. £25 every week on dry cleaning, for example, is going to work out at about £1,250 a year. This increased awareness of where all your money goes will perform miracles on your spending habits.

○ Go through the tips in Part 3 of this book and start applying them to your life. Remember that £5, £15 or £50 here or there could easily add up to £3,000 a year.

"If you are surrounded by more things than you can manage, you feel a weakness on a subliminal level. This feeling can

transfer to other areas of life in which you would otherwise be fully effective. Clutter impairs your development, because things that are piled up are frequently associated with memories, so they bind you to the past."

**'How to Simplify Your Life',
Tiki Kustenmacher and Lothar Seiwart**

RULE NO. 3:
'RESCUING THE ESSENTIAL FROM THE CLUTCHES OF THE IRRELEVANT'*

Wish you had an extra £500 a month coming in or a rich aunty to pay off your mortgage? Wish you could just have £2,000 to spend on yourself for a change, a new kitchen or brand new solid beech built-in wardrobes?

It's so easy to always fix your mind on things you wish you could have instead of appreciating how much you already have in your life. We are so crazily fixed on constantly improving on where we currently are in life that we fail to recognise the amazing place we have already reached.

I don't want to sound like your mother telling you to think of the children in poor countries when you wouldn't eat your spaghetti hoops, but it is actually very good for your own sense of contentment to remind yourself just how lucky you are from time to time.

○ Have a good long look at the home and life you have around you. Wander from room to room appreciating objects that are stylish and beautiful – the wood of your table, the pictures on the wall, that rug in the hall. Realise the amount of space you

---

*Title borrowed from 'Your Money or Your Life', Joe Dominguez and VickiRobin.

have and the amazing degree of comfort, luxury and security. Go through your wardrobe and handle the great items of clothing that you already own.

O Put by five minutes at the end of each day to sit down and appreciate all the positive joy you have in your life – be it your kids, your partner, the stew you're having, your tea, or that moment when your life was lit up by a robin in a hedge, or the warm touch of your wife before you dashed out of the door.

O Slow down and enjoy every second of life more. Enjoy and reclaim the simple pleasures in life – the act of cutting a loaf of bread, the feel of a porcelain cup or brushing your child's hair.

"A frugal person . . . might relish eating a single orange, enjoying the colour and texture of the whole fruit, the smell and the light spray that comes as you begin to peel it, the translucence of each section, the flood of the flavour . . . and the thrift of saving the peels for baking."

**'How to Simplify Your Life',
Tiki Kustenmacher and Lothar Seiwart**

O Tell yourself that you are wealthy and you will actually begin to realise it.

O Become lighter in everything you do or own. Enjoy having less in your drawers, less in your wardrobe, less in your food cupboards, less in your car. Your unconscious mind is weighed down by everything you own. It stores up knowledge of everything you own. Whatever things you have in your home, you also carry round in your head.

"The more you have, the less you are."

Karl Marx

RULE NO. 4:
DON'T BUY NEW IF YOU CAN BEG, BORROW, STEAL OR GO WITHOUT

Many years ago when I spent some time living in China, I was amazed by the number of different musical shouts and calls that would fill the air every few hours, each alerting me to a different hawker waiting for customers at the bottom of our block of flats. A certain cry denoted the baked sweet potato seller, another for the lady with a wooden bucket full of eels. But my favourite cry of all was for the man who came round to mend holes in people's saucepans.

Today in Britain it can cost more to get somebody to mend or alter a pair of trousers than to go to Matalan and buy a new pair. Yet it is exactly this trend that is leading to a decrease in quality, a lack of real appreciation for our possessions and a country that is splitting at the sides with all our landfill waste.

○ Before you reach for your credit card to buy a new sewing machine, bike or massage table or the like, ask around your friends and relatives to see if anyone has one you can borrow – or buy off them cheaply. If you asked me right now, for example, I would have each of these objects lying sadly unused in my shed and cupboards and would gladly loan them. The lesson is this: for many of the purchases that you might want to make, you'd be surprised how often a friend would actually be *very glad* to loan it to you.

○ Buy second hand. Shop for what you want at charity shops, car boot sales or on eBay. Answer those ads you see in the local papers. Develop a love for salvaging the old, reusing the beautiful, and bargain hunting on sunny frosty mornings.

○ Pool your resources. A group of friends or neighbours, for example, could easily share a pool of garden tools, kids' toys or even a tent, bike, car or holiday caravan.

○ Buy things that were built to last – instead of the cheapest thing available. Like a sturdy pair of walking boots, a wooden family salad bowl, and the nicer garden shears that won't go rusty.

○ Hire or rent when it will work out cheaper (such as cars, tools, holiday homes and wedding dresses). Always consider last year's models for things such as washing machines, pushchairs and V-neck jumpers.

○ And remember, a lot more things can be mended or recycled than you might imagine. Broken zips on clothes, bags and boots can easily be replaced. Greying white towels can be dyed a new colour. An old Etch-A-Sketch can be turned into a trendy frame to hang your photos in.

"If we can't make it ourselves you can't have it."

My father (who has built his own sheds and walls, kept the fires burning on salvaged wood and lives for a love of music)

RULE NO. 5:
CULTIVATE AN ENJOYMENT OF ELEGANT FRUGALITY

Most people fall victim to the common misconception that spending will make them feel rich. The truth, however, is that spending actually makes us feel poorer and out of control with our finances. Worse still, *the stress of mounting debt and overdrafts can send many of us into a panic that actually makes us spend even more instead of less.* It is often when we are already sliding into the red that we lose control of our spending.

One of the best feelings you can have, however, is having a bank account that is constantly a few thousand pounds in the black. And the weird thing is that keeping yourself at that kind of level really can make you spend less – and enjoy not doing it. Even if you are a compulsive spender today who loves nothing more than going on a shopping spree, you'll be amazed by how quickly you can completely reverse the tables and become a lover of frugality, saving money and *not spending*.

The feeling of wearing the same pair of boots for the fourth winter season in a row (re-heeled and re-soled and nicely polished) can be far better, deeper and longer-lasting than blowing £300 that you didn't have on a new pair. Learning to do your own DIY plumbing will make you feel very truly clever and save you hundreds of pounds into the bargain. And you can get a very special thrill from managing to feed a whole family of four on £50 for the week without scrimping on fruit or vegetables.

- As you go about your life over the next few months, slowly cultivate an enjoyment of spending less instead of more. Go to the shops less so that you have fewer opportunities to spend money. Feel virtuous when you don't buy something or opt for the cheaper option. With everything that you feel like buying ask yourself, "Do I really need that?" and realise that often the happy answer is "no".
- Feel proud of creating beauty in your home and happiness in your family – with a smaller amount of money but a larger amount of individuality, creativity, satisfying hard work and very good taste. Think darned antique linen tablecloths instead of brand new ones from Heales. A jam-jar full of bluebells picked in the woods. Your favourite Jimi Hendrix record turned into a clock. Leather elbow patches on the jumper you wear to smoke a pipe in your garden.
- Instead of buying things as soon as you want them, get in the habit of delaying gratification. The more you wait for something, the more you will enjoy it. Also, if you buy it straight away, it will only be a matter of a few weeks if not days before you start longing for something else (and probably better). It's against all the logic we're fed as consumers but the amazing truth is that buying 5 really lovely new things in a year will actually give you a lot more pleasure than buying 20.

○ Beware of impulse buys. These include buying things you really *want* at the time but will probably hardly ever use; almost anything you pick up while waiting at the cash till and buying no end of crazy things at Christmas because you've had a bit too much sherry (or nagging).

○ Remember the joy of saving up for things. When I was young, we lived on a farm where a lovely old chestnut mare lived in a stable right next to our kitchen window. When my grandfather decided to sell her, she was bought by the girl who delivered the milk for her father – with a shoe box full of one hundred £1 notes she'd been saving from her milk-round money. Whenever I remember that story, it actually makes me want to have *less money* instead of more!

○ Enjoy being thrifty. Make it an obsession. Make it something to inspire you and be proud of.

> *"Only the individual taste, in the end, can truly create style or fashion, since it is not concerned with following in the wake of others. Hence, whatever an individual taste may choose, be it a stepladder or a wicker basket, it must always be based on a deep personal choice, a spiritual need that truly assesses and gives value to that particular ladder or basket. The beauty of these things is somehow transmitted through the personality of the one who chooses. It is on our selection, after all, that we betray our deepest selves, and the individualist can make us see the objects of his choice with new eyes, with his eyes."*

Cecil Beaton

RULE NO. 6:
FIND YOUR OWN PERSONAL FINANCIAL
BLACK HOLES AND WEAKNESSES

Addicted to buying records, shoes or spending £20 on booze every night? Lifestyle aspirations bigger than your salary? Or are you simply 'not very good with money'?

In fact, for many people, some form of the above three is probably partly to blame for their overspending. You may already be aware of (some of) your own personal weaknesses, but there may be other black holes and defects that you are totally oblivious of, or somehow believe are unavoidable.

The important thing here is to become aware of where your money really goes and why – *and decide to do something about it*. One of the amazing things about human psychology is how we can spend years of our life suffering a problem, without really doing something to solve it. Sure, we'll fool ourselves into believing that we've tried to solve it, yet our blatant lack of a result quickly gives the lie to that deception. And it is the necessity of change that is important.

Over the next couple of weeks, spend some time having a really hard look at what you spend your money on and also both the practical and psychological reasons for your spending. Are you paying money out on credit card interest, for example, when you could actually afford to pay it off? *Is spending a compensation for having to work so hard*– or for something lacking in your childhood? Or are you simply spending too much on expensive food, gadgets, your home, schools or childcare for the children?

○ It is sometimes hard to spot our own weaknesses ourselves. Ask your partner and friends what they see as your personal money weaknesses. If you're really brave, consider asking a parent or consulting anyone else of an older generation.

○ Can you continue to afford the life you are leading without expecting your current income to rise over the next few years? Are you happy with the amount of money that goes out at the moment? If not, you might want to seriously consider doing something to change your spending. If your income does rise, then that will be brilliant. But the truth is that however much enjoyment you get from spending, the stress of not being able to make ends meet does mean that it might not actually be worth it.

○ *Find solutions.* Spend too much on CDs or trainers? Then put yourself on a monthly or yearly allowance. Spend too much on wine? Put limits on your weekly consumption or budget and/or buy wine for no more than £5 a bottle. Spend a fortune on your car and petrol? Trade down for a smaller car that hardly burns any petrol. Too much debt and mortgage? Consider seeking advice.

○ Bear in mind that sometimes the reasons why we overspend or want to buy things can be psychological or emotional. People tend to be more materialistic, for example, if they had non-nurturing parents, if they are insecure in life or suffer high levels of anxiety. Also consider the fact that you inherit much of your attitude towards money from your parents.

○ Can't bear to go a day without the warmth or satisfaction of spending money on something? Feel that the weekend is empty if you haven't had a chance to go out shopping? Consider these two comments by compulsive buyers in a study by Ronald Faber and Thomas O'Guinn:

"It's not that I wanted it, because sometimes, I'll just buy it and I'll think, 'Ugh, another sweatshirt?'"

"I can never go even to the [grocery store] and buy one quart of milk. I've always got to buy two."

Are you addicted to money:

"When we become addicted to money, it takes the place of emotions, replacing people as our primary focus and thus becoming more important than relationships. There is no room in our lives for anything but accumulating and holding onto our drug of choice."

**'Our Money Ourselves:
Redesigning Your Relationship with Money',
Dr C. Diane Ealy and Dr Kay Lesh**

RULE NO. 7:
ALWAYS REMEMBER THAT IT IS ABOUT HAVING MORE RATHER THAN LESS

This book, as I've said before, is not about going without or living the life of a pauper. The aim is to reduce your spending or outgoings while actually improving the quality of your life – both externally and internally.

Spending less and living better, for example, may mean driving a van through France for a week and buying cheap antique furniture, instead of spending £3,000 on a table in Linea Rosa because you haven't got the time to consider a more beautiful alternative.

Spending less and living better could mean replacing an expensive meal out on a Wednesday with a £8 life drawing class. A holiday in a cottage in Scotland instead of a week in Milan. Sardines from the market instead of monk fish from Marks and Spencer. Or putting tap water and cheap squash through a soda stream instead of spending £20 a month on cans of pop for the kids or San Pellegrino water for your dinner guests.

○ Whatever you decide to economise on, remember that it's not about doing without but about choosing something better. Afternoon tea at a posh hotel instead of a much more expensive swanky lunch meal. A single but exotic flower on the table instead of a showy and overpriced bouquet. Carefree shoes for £25 instead of stress-inducing ones at £250. Living on a barge instead of a stressful life in the city.

○ Always remember to make space for yourself. Don't let a preoccupation with money obscure you. You won't get to the end of your life and wish you'd made more money – you'll wish you spent more time staring at the clouds, travelling the world, playing with your children, or doing something more meaningful.

○ Remember that the less you spend, the wealthier you will feel – as you suddenly realise you've actually saved up loads of money. The more creative you are with your spending, the greater the satisfaction. Live wisely and slowly and you will feel very clever!

○ Stop wishing that you had more money and feel proud of the amount of money you earn instead. You work hard to earn every penny, so carry that pride on to the way that you spend it. And the way you live your life.

Don't do a job you hate just to finance a lifestyle that is a compensation for the work you have to do in the first place.

"The moment one gives close attention to anything, even a blade of grass, it becomes a mysterious, awesome, indescribably magnificent world in itself."

Henry Miller

PART 3

THE TACTICS

365 ways to spend less while improving the
quality of your life

9

SHOPPING

○ Why B&Q will do anything to make you go shopping
○ How to spend less on everything you buy
○ How to spend 30% less a year without even noticing it

It is 17th November. I do not believe in shopping for Christmas too early. Yet when an advert comes on TV for B&Q's Christmas shopping day with 10% off throughout the store, some kind of flicker of a feeling does temporarily come over me and I think: "Perhaps we should go to that?"

And that's how they get you.

Lying on the sofa at the end of the day with few brain cells or energy left for anything resembling rational thought. And the poor souls who did go to that sale would have come back with £120 worth of icicle-shaped lights for the Christmas tree, naff felt stockings for the kids, spray snow for the window, a wiggly-headed laughing Rudolph novelty toy and a light-up snowman for the garden. None of which they had ever needed or wanted. And even though they couldn't work out how a few really bargain purchases of less than a fiver each could come to so much money overall, at least it was all at a 10% discount.

Whoopeedee.

Because shopping, you see, is what it's all about.

Just hours after thousands of innocent Americans and the world's tallest twin skyscrapers were brought to the ground by kamikaze pilots on 11th September, George Bush addressed the nation in his first speech after the tragedy and said:

> *"If you love your country, if you want to fight terrorism,*
> *go out this weekend and . . . shop!"*

For, as Paco Underhill says in 'Why We Buy: The Science of Shopping':

> *"If we went into stores only when we needed to buy*
> *something, and if once there we bought only what we needed,*
> *the economy would collapse."*

The truth is that the more time you spend in shops, the more money you will spend. And the shops will employ every cunning trick in the book to get you through the door.

Follow these tips and I *guarantee* you will spend at least 30% less over the coming months, *without even noticing it*.

SHOP LESS

The less time you spend in shops, the less money you will spend. So just stop shopping. Always remember that the main aim of any big store owner is to get you through the door. Once they've got you there, they know you will spend some money.

Spend a few hours walking around the shops on a Saturday and you're bound to buy something. Pop into Marks & Spencer for a meal for the evening and you may not make it back without spending less than £50 on groceries – not to mention the toy you bought impulsively on your way to the food section.

○ Shop less.
○ Shop more sparingly.
○ Shop in cheaper shops that you aren't particularly fond of instead of the hell holes of temptation that have you wishing you could have everything on the shelves.

Remember: If you don't see it, you won't buy it.

1 MAKE A SHOPPING LIST

Be it Tesco, B&Q, clothes shopping or a trip to Ikea, don't leave the house before writing a list of what it is that you're after. Don't allow yourself to fill your basket full of other things you might as well get just because you've seen them. Or allow yourself only a set number of such extra purchases – be it 1, 2, 3 or 4. And don't allow the emotional side of yourself to dupe the rational side of you with the argument that it will save money in the long run.

Remember this shopping fact from Paco Underhill's files: *"Two-thirds of supermarket purchases are unplanned."* Write a list before you go and try to stick to it. Don't just pull things off the shelves impulsively.

2 IS SHOPPING A PASTIME?

Don't make a habit of shopping as a hobby, leisure activity or way of filling the hours of the weekend (or weekday if you're a stay-at-home parent). Replace those activities with more positive, real or healthy pursuits instead. Be it rock climbing, kite flying or mending old bicycles, finding new things to do with your spare time will help you spend less money by reducing the time you spend shopping. It also works because the fulfilment that your new pastime gives you will reduce your need to fill your life with material goods instead.

3 *DON'T SHOP WHEN YOU'RE A BIT TIPSY OR ON AN EMOTIONAL HIGH*

You will spend far more than a more sober you and will regret it afterwards.

4 *DO I REALLY NEED THIS?*

Before you allow yourself to put anything in the basket, other than dog food and toilet rolls, get in the habit of asking yourself a few key questions. Anything along the lines of "Do I really, really need this?" will probably do the job. You will get to the point where you will actually feel a lot better not buying instead of buying.

> Remember that what you actually want is less stuff in your life, not more.

5 *SHOP LESS FOR A CALMER LIFE*

Psychologist Barry Schwartz, in his book 'The Paradox of Choice', argues that too much choice can leave us bemused and unhappy. He wonders whether we really need the 275 varieties of cereal and 175 salad dressings he found in his supermarket. Realise that you won't necessarily be reducing your happiness if you restrict the amount of time you spend in the Aladdin's caves that pass as food shops and department stores these days.

6 GET THE BEST AND CHEAPEST ON ALL MAJOR ITEMS

Need to buy a new vacuum cleaner, washing machine or laptop? Don't just go to the shops and buy what you fancy, or the best that money can buy. In many cases, it is not true that you get what you pay for. The cheaper options can often actually be the better models. If you go to the *Which?* magazine website (www.which.co.uk), you can get a free 30-day trial that will allow you to access reports on whatever kind of object it is you're after buying – from calcium supplements and breakfast cereals through to DVDs and TVs. Buy something that will work better and last longer and it could save you several hundreds of pounds each time. Take a washer-drier, for example. *Which?* say that the Zanussi-Electrolux ZWD1480W is the only model that dries as well as a tumble dryer. Hoover washing machines come the lowest in reliability – a 1 in 3 chance of going wrong in the first six years. This information is worth knowing.

7 HUNT FOR A CHARITY SHOP WITH APPLIANCES

Some charity shops specialise in electrical items, from kettles and toasters to larger appliances like washing machines and fridges. They are cheaper than the brand new versions and you can also feel safe with the knowledge that they have all been tested for health and safety.

8 CHANGE THE WAY YOU THINK ABOUT SHOPPING

Need some groceries – go to the supermarket. Need some presents – hunt in the gift department. Need a new coat – go to a department store. Most of us shop according to a formula, yet we could get so much more from our shopping as well as our money if we just tried to think out of the box more often.

While taking a walk in London once, for example, I came across an Ephemera Fair and went inside for a browse. I came out with a 1940's pencil drawing done by a serviceman of his girlfriend for £2. It made the perfect moving-in gift for a friend.

Need a new coat? Try a second-hand designer store. Need a new waste-paper basket? Look in bric-a-brac stores for something really original. Need some honey? How about buying it from a local beekeeper?

9 TRY DELAYING GRATIFICATION

Instead of allowing yourself to impulse buy when you see something you like, only allow yourself to have it if you are prepared to make the effort to return to the shop at a later occasion.

10 SAVE CASH AND THE PLANET

We may think that certain things that we buy are 'cheap' and that we are therefore justified in buying them as part of a money-saving strategy. There are two things wrong with this equation, however.

○ First of all, it is often the very fact that things are cheap that tricks us into buying things we never actually need.
○ Secondly, these things may appear to be a good deal from a purely financial perspective. Damage done to the environment, not to mention the general moral fibre of the world that we live in, however, is not costed in.

The surprising thing that you might not be expecting is that buying more ethically can actually save you money. The last time *Ethical Consumer* magazine surveyed clothing retailers, for example, it found that the best codes of practice came from Monsoon, H&M and Matalan. Other companies that you might call 'cheap and cheerful' such as New Look and Marks & Spencer are members of the Ethical Trade Initiative.

11 BECOME A COMMITTED BARGAIN-HUNTER

Start learning how to get everything cheaper and shop around for the cheapest price for everything. Take advantage of the 2-for-1 offers at supermarkets. Go to Topshop for a new jumper instead of Aquascutum. Visit online sites which tell you the cheapest place where you can find the objects you're looking for, such as:

○ www.kelkoo.co.uk
○ www.pricerunner.co.uk
○ www.shopzilla.co.uk

(12) CHEAP SHOPS CAN MAKE YOU SPEND MORE

I was tempted to give you the details of a guide you can buy that lists all the bargain shops and factory outlets, etc., throughout the country. I actually believe, however, that giving you access to this list could make you spend more! You already know that going shopping is the fastest way to part with your money. Going shopping for bargains is just as bad, if not worse, because you can justify your shopping as sensible if it's cheaper.

(13) AVOID THE BUYING FRENZY

Also remember the secret that retailers love, which I call *buying euphoria*. The thrill of buying one thing will make you want to buy more. Let yourself buy those trousers and shirts, and you may suddenly find yourself losing all reason and buying up half the shop. Order a sofa in Habitat and you may find yourself almost dancing through the shop buying other things. Be aware of the power of the buying frenzy and don't let it get the better of you.

(14) SHOPO ONLINE

Not only do you tend to get lower prices buying online, it also means that you're not in a shop surrounded by other objects that you can pick up and buy. This may not work for you if you're the kind of person who likes spending a lot of time surfing, as it could have the reverse effect. Only you know yourself.

(15) RECOGNISE YOUR OWN WEAKNESSES

For example, make sure you're not using your kids as an excuse for spending. I for one love buying things and spending money, but have managed to dramatically curb my spending on myself. I can sometimes let it slip, however, by buying things for my kids. After all, what could be more innocent, beautiful and loving than wanting to buy your children some books when you're in Waterstones?

 ACT LIKE IT IS YOUR JOB TO SAVE MONEY

Apply the same principles of cost-cutting to your own personal life as you do in your job. A friend of mine who works in publishing, for example, realised that he will phone six different companies for quotes on a printing job, yet pay the first price he's given on anything he buys for himself. Or at least he did before he realised what he'd been doing. Men also tend to dislike shopping so much that they will do anything (and pay anything) to have it over and done with quicker.

 BEWARE OF SHOP ASSISTANTS

One of my favourite stories about the art of selling is about two old brothers who owned a gentlemen's clothes store in New York. When a customer came in, one brother (obviously somewhat hard of hearing) would attend to them while the other busied himself in a different part of the shop. After the customer had tried on a suit, he would normally enquire about the price. The first brother would then call to the other brother asking him what the price of the suit was. "Seventy dollars," the first would reply. "That one is just seventeen dollars," the second would then report to the customer. "Just seventeen dollars?" the customer would ask, making sure he had got it right. And then he would snap up that fifteen dollar suit for seventeen and bolt out of the shop as quickly as his legs would take him.

I'm not of course suggesting that shop assistants today will use tricks that are quite as deceitful as this. But they do use tricks – after all, a lot of them are on commission. If you are offered a discount on something, for example, don't feel that you are now obliged to buy it. Also don't allow shop assistants to make you spend more than you had intended because you are too embarrassed to say that a price is more than you want to pay. In my experience, in fact, it is the people with more money who are more likely to say things like this. Feel more confident in these situations by previously deciding on a phrase that you feel comfortable saying. "I have a rule of never spending more than £50 on shirts", "I'll get into too much trouble if I do" or "I think I'll go to Primark", for example, are all legitimate responses.

(18) DON'T LET THEM UPSELL YOU TO A PRICIER MODEL

Beware of any shop assistant who tries to upsell you to a more expensive option by explaining all its better features and benefits. Try and stick to the cheap option you wanted to buy.

(19) BEWARE OF BARGAINS

If you love bargains, shops love you. When shopping, never buy anything just because it's a 'real bargain'. Never buy something because you get something else free or for half-price. Beware of picking up anything because you happen to see it while you're waiting at the tills.

Bargains are used as bait. Remember that lower pricing or 'value' are just other ways of getting you in the store. So while you may be saving money by buying a £17 pair of jeans from George at Asda, you may not save money in the long run. By the time you come out, you may have found you've spent another £50 on a selection of items you didn't even realise you needed before you went in.

20) CHOOSE YOUR SUPERMARKET CAREFULLY

Luxury food items are a big temptation, and a big drain on your budget. I always remember when the new Sainsburys came to town and everybody started shopping there. A couple of months later, my cousin told me that he and his girlfriend had decided to stop shopping at the new Shopping Heaven and return to Gateway (now Somerfield) because they were spending so much more on their groceries.

21) AVOID BRANDED GOODS

Be aware that branded goods – such as Diesel jeans, Elle MacPherson underwear or Jamie Oliver saucepans – are one of the retail industry's favourite ways of making you spend loads of money on things that only cost them a few quid to make. In fact, they spend a lot more on the advertising that makes you yearn for these products than they do on actually producing them. Remember that branding is big business, designed to make you feel inadequate as a person unless you buy the right brands that will show the rest of the world what a cool kind of person you are. Non-branded products are normally just as good, if not better, quality – and will only cost you half the price.

(22) BEWARE OF SALES OR HALF-PRICE OFFERS

Sales can be a great way of getting what you need for a lower price, but only if you're a very careful and disciplined shopper. Not only might sales lure you into buying things you never needed or wanted in the first place, they might also be a bit of a con. *Which?* magazine, for example, discovered that MFI regularly used fake 'was' prices to make it seem that your 'Now 50% off' price was an amazing bargain. Sales in clothes shops are a great way for shops to offload duff clothes on bargain hunters blinded by the discount.

(23) BEWARE OF 'BUY NOW, PAY LATER' DEALS

Buy Now, Cry Later! Don't be tempted to take up offers of interest-free credit or 'Buy Now, Pay Later'. While the temptation to not have to lose the money now is very hard to resist, it will hurt more in the long run to pay for something after you've already had it or even lost or broken it. Also don't allow yourself to think that you will have more money to pay for it in six months' time, because you probably won't – especially if you've been delaying payment for other things as well.

(24) DON'T PICK UP A BASKET

Another interesting fact from retail anthropologist Paco Underhill is that *"Customers who pick up a basket nearly always buy something*". So don't pick up a basket! Even if you do end up buying something, you still won't be tempted to keep adding more and more things to your shopping trolley. Even the shopping trolleys that they have when you are shopping online are dangerous because they always make you feel compelled to buy more than one item.

25) AVOID BEING SOLD TO OVER THE PHONE

Fed up with telephone sales calls? Avoid ever being sold to (or conned) over the phone. Contact the *Telephone Preference Service* and they will put you on their list. If a telesales company wishes to make sales calls, they are legally obliged to exclude people who are on this list from their calls (phone 0845 0700707 or visit www.tpsonline.org.uk).

26) WATCH OUT FOR MUSEUM GIFT SHOPS

Another weak spot, especially for women: watch out for places such as museum gift shops, sweet shops and any shop you go into when you're on holiday. For some reason, both women and children find it very difficult to enter and exit this kind of establishment without actually buying something.

27) EXERCISE YOUR RIGHTS IF PRODUCTS DON'T LAST

Whenever you buy something from a shop, you have statutory rights under the Sale of Goods Act. This states that whatever you buy must be in good condition and free from faults and must last for a reasonable length of time. If a zip on a garment breaks, or a heel falls off a boot after just a few months of wear, take it back to the shop and ask for a refund or replacement item.

(28) KNOW YOUR ONLINE RIGHTS

You have the right to an automatic, no-questions refund if buying online. When you buy anything online, you are automatically protected under the Distance Selling Regulations. You can return anything for a refund within seven working days from the day after the goods are delivered. You don't need a reason and you simply have to cancel the order in writing within that period.

(29) CHECK SWAP XCHANGE

Check this website before you buy – or throw away – anything. Swap Xchange is a fantastic organisation that wants to encourage more and more people to "swap, exchange, find or give away ideas, goods or services that are no longer needed by you but that may be wanted by someone else". If you visit their website (www .swapxchange.org), you may be able to find exactly what you're looking for – to swap for something else or given away for free if you collect. On my visit to the site today, for example, I've noted a piano in exchange for some work on the garden, a free set of children's encyclopedias to anyone who will collect, several beds free to collectors and a Steely Dan signed guitar. The service is completely free and using it couldn't be easier. Either phone numbers or email addresses are given, so it's more like looking in a local newspaper than discovering that it's two in the morning and you're still on eBay.

30 DON'T FORGET YOUR LOCAL POUND SHOP

Are you making the most of your local pound shop? If you're the kind of person who needs to go shopping now and again, try letting off a bit of shopping steam in the local pound shop instead of the local department store. Everybody loves this Aladdin's cave shopping experience and you can come out with some very useful, and penny-saving, things. Keep a list of potential pound shop purchases that you need (coat hangers, glue, new washing line, waste paper basket, etc.) and then take a trip down there when you have a few things on your list.

31 GO TO THE MARKET

As with the pound shop, you can find bits and pieces for your house from your local market. What's more, you may stumble across industrial-sized household items that will last longer, such as clingfilm and kitchen foil.

32 HAGGLE FOR A CHEAPER PRICE

This is particularly effective in privately owned stores where you are talking directly to the owner or manager. They'll often be far happier to have a sale at 5% less than they're asking than not at all. In larger chain stores, always ask for a discount if you can see any faults at all in an item or its packaging.

33 GET A FREE PERSONAL SHOPPER

A lot of large department stores provide a personal shopping service for their customers. You may be surprised to find that this service is actually free – so a great way to get a bit of luxury and free refreshments for nothing. You are not, of course, obliged to buy anything. Ring ahead to make an appointment.

34 DON'T OVERSPEND AT CHRISTMAS

Christmas can be a very dangerous time of year because of the frenzy effect of buying. The act of making purchases, it seems, sets you off on a buying frenzy where all reason goes out the window and you just can't stop. Men may be particularly prone to simply throwing lots of money at the situation because it's their best attempt at getting the whole thing 'solved' or 'over'. Women are probably more likely to spend too much money on beautiful baubles or decorations – or spending a fortune on £5 items for everybody's stockings.

Every time you do any kind of shopping during the Christmas season, always ask yourself whether you really need everything in your basket, or whether you could make do instead with something cheaper or even free. Before you go to the checkout, make yourself return a couple of the things in the basket to help you sort out the unnecessary add-on purchases and impulse buys.

35 TRY SECRET SANTA

Persuade your friends, work colleagues, family or other social groups to take part in Secret Santa. Agree a limit on how much to spend, and it will also allow you more time to choose fewer presents, rather than rushing around trying to find something for everybody.

5 SAVE MONEY ON DECORATIONS

Instead of getting a fresh tree every year, get yourself a good quality plastic Christmas tree. Encourage your children to make their own decorations. You can also find perfectly usable discounted decorations in the January sales.

CLOTHES: HOW TO HAVE A FANTASTIC (OR AT LEAST SERVICEABLE) WARDROBE WITHOUT OVERSPENDING

7 SPEND WHAT MONEY YOU DO SPEND WISELY

Instead of blowing large amounts on extravagant items you may decide that you don't actually like later, spend your money on clothes that you can wear every day instead.

8 MEN: SPEND JUST TEN MINUTES LONGER

Be aware that when a man takes clothing into a dressing room, the only thing that is likely to prevent him from buying it is if it doesn't fit. Some men will even buy things without trying them on and then dump them at the back of the wardrobe because they don't fit.

9 MEN: HOW NOT TO PROVE YOUR VIRILITY

Referring again to extensive research done by Paco Underhill and his researchers, following and observing thousands of people shopping, about a third of men don't actually look at price tags. It is almost, Paco suggests, a measure of their virility.

(40) WOMEN: DON'T SHOP WITH A FRIEND

You are statistically more likely to spend a lot more.

(41) BE A TRENDSETTER NOT A TREND FOLLOWER

One of the most expensive things you can do when it comes to clothing is buying this season's most fashionable items. If everyone's wearing it this year, you certainly won't want to be seen dead in it next year. Instead of buying fashionable items, look for clothes that you really love but are not the latest hot fashion. You'll look more individual and will be able to wear and enjoy these beautiful items for years to come.

(42) BUY ITEMS THAT MATCH

When you see a top you like, ask yourself if you already have trousers to go with it at home. Don't buy a bag just because it's pretty – if it doesn't work with any of your outfits, you are less likely to use it. This thinking will also help if you have the tendency to buy accessories like new shoes and jewellery every time you buy new clothes.

(43) GO ON HOLIDAY TO THAILAND AND HAVE CLOTHES MADE BY TAILORS THERE

If you do it properly, you could save money in total – including the cost of the holiday! Take clothes to be copied or buy patterns before you go out.

4 SAVILE ROW SUITS AT A THIRD OF THE PRICE

There is a company called *James and James* that will make you a properly tailored suit at a fraction of the price – a mere £750. Because everything is done online, you can choose your own fabric and the style of your suit and take your own measurements (following their careful online instructions) at your own leisure and without having to make a trip to their Savile Row shop. Their customers include leaders of industry, politicians and show business personalities. You can even have an exact replica made for you of the suit worn by the Duke of Windsor, a former customer.

5 GET CLOTHES MADE BY A LOCAL SEAMSTRESS

Ask at the dry cleaners to see if they can recommend somebody, or look for adverts in local shops or papers. Choose your own pattern and material or ask to have a favourite item copied.

6 BORROW OUTFITS FOR SPECIAL OCCASIONS

Try to avoid buying too many items of clothing for 'going out' or special occasions, if you don't think you'll get much use out of them. See if you can borrow clothes from friends for weddings or special nights out – then they can borrow items from you too to expand their wardrobe.

7 BUY TIMELESS ITEMS IN THE JANUARY SALES

Instead of rushing out to buy a new winter coat or suit in October, for example, hold out till January (when the cold weather actually really starts), and it will be a better bargain as well as a nice pick-me-up for the dark months at the beginning of the year.

48 DON'T BUY CLOTHES THAT ARE TOO SMALL

Don't buy clothes that are too small in the hope you'll be able to fit into them when you're slimmer. Even as an incentive to lose weight, this is proven not to work. If you buy clothes that are the right size then you will feel better about yourself and that will help you lose weight. Trying to fit into clothes that are too small will make you feel bad about yourself, which will in turn make you more likely to put on weight or have trouble dieting.

49 HOW TO LOOK BRILLIANT EVERY DAY

There are a number of people that I have met in my life who have stuck in my mind for sheer enviable brilliance in certain areas. In the sartorial area, I always remember the sister of a certain ex of my father who looked amazing, yet wore exactly the same outfit every day. A crisp white T-shirt (several on rotation, regularly bleached and carefully ironed), black leggings (she was very tall and thin and dyed three pairs black on a regular basis), black braces and a pair of black thigh-length boots. I am not suggesting that you copy this outfit exactly, but that a similar technique could be adapted that would set you apart as a unique individual and be the perfect answer to outstanding sartorial achievement on a minimum budget.

50) GET CLOTHES MENDED

Elbow patches on lovely old jumpers, I hear, are very fashionable these days. As are beautifully repaired holes in gloves, blouses and trousers. You might not want to wear such items to an important interview but they'll give you a much sought-after air of shabby chic elegance elsewhere. It will also make your favourite items of clothing survive a lot longer. If you can't do it yourself or persuade somebody else to do it for you, you could always ask at your dry cleaners.

51) PROTECT YOUR CLOTHES FROM DAMAGE

Make sure you don't lose much-loved or expensive items of clothing to unnecessary damage. Don't cook or paint in good clothes, for example, and make sure that woollens in particular are protected from moths.

10

HOUSE AND HOME

○ How to stick to your dreams but keep them more within your means

○ Spend £1,000 – 100,000 less

You most probably spend more money on your home or accommodation than on anything else. So surely it makes sense, therefore, to look here for money-saving opportunities. But how is that possible?

To a large extent, of course, that will depend on where you're coming from. And possibly more so than for any other chapter in this book, this will differ quite wildly from reader to reader.

Perhaps you are someone looking for a change in their life. Maybe you are seriously struggling to make ends meet. Or perhaps you just wish you had more money left at the end of the month to buy that gorgeous sofa, new pair of speakers, or bit of land for a pony.

And manage you shall. Because I really do believe that you will find the lifestyle that will make you happy.

Only it may just take a bit of rethinking.

A SENSE OF PROPORTION

While interviewing people during research for this book, I gradually realised that something rather odd was going on when it came to people's attitudes to the money they spend on accommodation. It almost seemed that this was not seen as an expense at all, but something completely necessary. And not only was it necessary to spend enormous amounts of money on your home, but for the vast majority of people, it was actually unquestionable that you would do anything other than buying the most expensive house you could afford, borrowing the absolute highest amount of money that the building societies would lend you.

I talked to people, for example, who were very eager to know how they could spend less on a loaf of bread or a breast of chicken, yet were spending thousands of pounds every month on their mortgage. I spoke to others who were already very smart at borrowing things they needed or getting cheap socks for the kids, yet had spent far more than they could afford on their home.

Why?

Maybe because we're British. Maybe because property is so darned expensive. Or maybe because of this growth-obsessed way of thinking we have that says we must always be getting richer, always going upwards. Always able to afford bigger and better.

And are we likely to change?

Probably not very much. There should, however, be some ideas amidst the following that will help you stick to your dreams but keep them more within your means. You should certainly be able to save a minimum of £1,000 – either now or in the future – and easily as much as £100,000.

If you can't afford the home you really want (including if you've already bought it), then you are going to have to change something in the picture slightly.

52 THINK OUTSIDE THE BOX

Whether you're in the process of buying or just considering a move, try to open your options out as wide as possible. It is a natural human trait to always try to look for a solution or a change of circumstance within a very small or limited field of possibilities. So, instead of getting out the local paper and looking through the property pages, sit yourself in front of a map of the whole of the UK – or beyond. Find out how much property costs in Devon or Canterbury or Hastings or the countryside of Scotland. There's no reason why you wouldn't be able to find your dream home and lifestyle in a town at the opposite end of the country – if you are prepared to move there. You may be pleasantly surprised to discover that you can get just the job you want in just the place you want to be. And maybe earn more money and get more job satisfaction.

And it isn't just location . . .

53 BE PREPARED TO LET SOMETHING GO

If your criteria includes two bathrooms, detached, with off-street parking, you'll certainly be able to find a much cheaper – and probably better – property if you let one of your criteria drop. Be prepared to park on the street and you might find that the properties that now appear in your price range are actually far more appealing than everything you'd been looking at before. Even being prepared to move a few streets down from the area you're currently looking in could make a large difference in price.

(54) GET A HOUSE FOR £1

In the UK, there are over a million empty properties – many of which you could buy for as little as £1, especially if the local council is trying to regenerate the area. In some areas you can even get a grant to help you with the renovation.

www.Empro.co.uk is a government-sponsored website that lists empty homes in West London. In other areas, you could try contacting the local council for a list of empty properties, or just look around for derelict properties yourself.

If you do find a derelict property that you'd be interested in buying, contact the Land Registry first to find out who owns it, or ring the council to see whether they have it on their list. Another way to find properties 'in need of modernisation' is through local auctions. Often the owner is forced to sell because the council takes out a compulsory purchase order, and must sell it immediately for whatever price they can get.

Rescuing a deserted property like this can be an amazing way to get a great house you really love for much, much less than you'd otherwise have had to pay for it. It can, of course, also be a time-consuming process to repair and renovate, and it is advisable to get a survey followed by quotes from builders where necessary to find out how much the refurbishment will cost.

55) GET PAID £150,000 TO BE A PROPERTY DEVELOPER

Another option to consider is that the renovation of a dilapidated house could become a full-time job for a year. If you end up getting yourself a £300,000 house for £150,000, for example, that could be a lot better use of your time than commuting into the office every day. Apply yourself to learning some of the techniques of the trade and you could even become an expert in plastering, plumbing or interior design by the end of it.

56) DON'T LIVE IN LONDON

Don't live in London – it's too expensive and you have a lower quality of life. In the Mercer's 2004 Cost of Living survey, London ranked as the second most expensive city in the world, measured by the cost of over 200 items including housing, food, clothing, transport and entertainment. In the Mercer Quality of Life survey – based on 39 key quality of life factors including housing, health services, schools and recreation facilities – London ranked 35th.

57) LOOK FOR SOMETHING CHEAPER

Look for something cheaper – you might get something better. Next time you're looking for a place to buy, don't automatically just look at houses within a certain budget – in other words, the most you can afford plus the £20,000–50,000 you add on when the estate agent asks you what your limit is. Instead, also look at properties that cost £30,000–100,000 less than you were thinking of paying; you may just be surprised.

58 CONSIDER SCALING DOWN

Sell your current home and buy something cheaper and you could suddenly be rich beyond your wildest dreams.

And if that doesn't make any sense at first, think about it again. If you're paying less for the home in which you live, you will have more to spend on everything else instead. OK, to a certain extent you can see the logic behind thinking that the larger a property you own, the wealthier you are, but that is only true if you actually own it, and only if you can afford it. Mortgages have a lot to answer for – the enormous rise in the price of property included.

Is it *really* worth stretching yourself so far to buy the biggest and best house you can by taking the very most that the mortgage lenders will lend you? Would you be happier and less stressed out by your finances if you bought something more within your means?

59 TRY AUCTIONS

Ever wondered about buying a property at auction? It can certainly be an amazing way to find a bargain, as long as you stay level-headed. Every year in the UK some 600 property auctions are conducted countrywide, yet very few private home owners actually buy their homes this way. So why let property developers and professionals get all the bargains while hardworking individuals like yourself get left paying over the odds?

Your first step is to request auction catalogues from auction houses in your local area – or in the area where you'd like to buy. Look in local papers, on the internet, the Yellow Pages or directory enquiries. The next step is to do your homework. Educate yourself with as much information as you can glean about how auctions work and the best way to get the best bargains. You need to understand, for example, why properties will often sell for a higher price than the 'guide price' and have your 10% deposit and mortgage set up before the auction. Spend time studying the prices of the kind of place you're after in all the areas you're interested in buying so you can be sure what price to pay. Always visit properties prior to any auction and seriously consider getting a full survey before you go ahead with any bidding.

Finally, if you do find a property that you're interested in, you need to telephone the auctioneer and tell him the 'Lot' number you're interested in, whether or not you've had a survey, and that you have prepared your finances. Make sure you have a solicitor ready to act for you, then get to the auction house early with everything you might need to carry out the purchase. Remember that when you make a bid at auction, you are making an unconditional and binding offer.

CONSIDER LIVING OVERSEAS

Imagine if you could pay just £300 a month in rent for a large villa with views across the sea in a country where it's always warm and the oranges are enormous. And imagine if you could earn a UK wage while living there.

It may sound like a pipe dream but it really is possible. I know of one person, for example, who earns a high wage creating websites for UK companies, yet pays very little for food and accommodation in his two homes in Portugal and the

Czech Republic. I know of a copywriter who works for companies in Germany yet lives with his family in Honduras. Some other acquaintances work from a wonderful rural home in the Scottish Highlands and need only do a few hours work a week to support themselves.

61 ENJOY FREE ACCOMMODATION

This certainly won't appeal to or be practical for everybody, but think for a minute about how you could live your life and what you could do in your life if you didn't have to pay any rent or a mortgage. Whether it's a permanent lifetime plan or just a way of getting away from it all for a few months or a year, there are many ways of getting free accommodation. You could even take up this option while renting out your current home.

Think very, very hard and ask around to see if you can find somewhere to live for free for a year or part of the year. Do you have an aunt with a caravan, for example? A friend of a friend with a holiday home in Spain sat vacant for the winter? A cousin with a barge or a semi-derelict farm building? Or just a parent or relative who'd be happy to put you up for some time? Ask around and you may be surprised by what you find and the offers you receive.

Squatting is still a legal means of getting accommodation without having to pay for it. For some it is a necessity, for others it forms part of a lifestyle choice. Either way, if you can get into an empty building without doing any damage, you can make it your home. You can even have the right to rubbish collection, postal delivery, social security, water and electricity. All you need to do is find the right kind of place and you may even be able to stay there for several years.

You can find out more – including how to change locks and deal with visiting police or officials – in the 'Squatters Handbook'. Send a cheque for £2 to: Advisory Service for Squatters, 84b Whitechapel High St, London E1 7QX.

52) HOUSE SITTING

Enjoy a free holiday in other people's houses. Another great route for getting free accommodation, a change of scene or even just for the pleasure is by becoming a house and/or pet sitter. When people go away on holiday or to spend time at a second home, they often feel very anxious about leaving their homes empty or pets on their own. Many people therefore employ a house sitter – either directly or through an agency.

Agencies such as Safe Hands Sitters (www.safehandssitters. co.uk, Tel: 0845 2600 488), The Home Service (www.house sitters.co.uk, Tel: 08451 303100) and (www.housesitworld. com), take people on their books and then find them work. Alternatively you could try advertising either locally or through your own website yourself.

53) VOLUNTEER OVERSEAS FOR A YEAR

The organisation Voluntary Services Overseas (VSO) is always looking for volunteers with skills that can be used in developing countries. You go away for normally two years and receive accommodation and a local wage when you get there. It's one way of escaping the expensive cost of living in this country – and an amazing life-changing experience besides. Check out their website at www.vso.org.uk.

MORE WAYS OF SAVING OR MAKING MONEY WHENEVER YOU BUY OR SELL PROPERTY

(64) CHOOSING THE BEST TIME TO BUY OR SELL

The best time of the year to buy your home at a lower price is during the winter months. Far fewer people are looking during this time, so vendors can get desperate and drop their price or take a lower offer. For the same reason, trying to sell your home during the winter months may not be the best idea. In fact, figures show that April is the month when a glut of first-time buyers seem to go on a buying frenzy.

(65) MAKE YOUR HOUSE INSTANTLY MORE SALEABLE

People like to buy homes that are clean, odour-free and full of light. They do not like homes that are dimly lit, dirty or smelly. One of the best ways to add value to your home for free is to scrub it until it is spotless and open up all the windows to blast air through it before you show people round. Clean windows. Tie back curtains to let in maximum light. Put 100 watt bulbs in everywhere.

(66) ADD REAL VALUE

What really adds value – and what doesn't? Generally, spending money on a new garage, loft conversion or building a new room or conservatory will normally add more value than the cost. Adding double glazing, costly features or a swimming pool will not.

57) DON'T FOOL YOURSELF

While updating an old kitchen or bathroom for a modern new one will almost always add value, don't allow yourself to use this excuse to justify spending £30,000 on the bathroom of your dreams. It probably won't add £30,000 in value. Any decent white bathroom suite with a bit of DIY tiling and/or decorating can be very effective without costing too much money.

58) SET YOURSELF A TIMESCALE OF A YEAR
TO FIND THE RIGHT PROPERTY FOR YOU

Most people, as soon as they've decided they want to move or buy, want it to happen as quickly as humanly possible. Unfortunately for them, however, it can be this rush that could lead them to pay far more than they might need to. If you can give yourself time to watch the market carefully and visit as many places as possible, you will stand a much better chance of finding the perfect property at a lower price.

59) LOOK BEYOND THE FORMICA

Try to see beyond an ugly surface. You have a much better chance of finding a bargain if you're prepared to take on a home 'in need of modernisation' or that has been strangely and unattractively decorated.

70 *BUY A FLAT OVER A SHOP*

It can be a really cheap way of buying more space for less –
plus you don't have anybody noisy living underneath you from
six in the evening. You will not, of course, want to buy over
a kebab or fish and chip shop. And obviously check out the
soundproofing during the day.

71 *PAY NO MORE THAN £49 – £500 IN FEES*
WHEN YOU SELL YOUR HOME

Don't want to pay an estate agent 2% of your sale price just
to take a few photographs and point out to prospective buyers
where your bathroom is? With most home buyers doing their
initial search for property online these days, you could save
yourself a lot of money by selling via one of the online estate
agents instead. Some charge as little as £49, others charge £99
plus 0.5% commission. It all depends on what kind of service
you want, and which of the major online property websites you
want to be listed on. www.rightmove.co.uk, for example, gets
the most visitors. Do a Google search for something like 'sell
home online' and look into the different options available.

72 *FLOG IT!*

Use the opportunity to get rid of all the clutter in your house.
There is probably a lot of junk in the loft that you haven't got
round to sorting out yet. Flog it on eBay or hold a garage or
car boot sale.

MORTGAGES

73 REDUCE THE COST OF YOUR MORTGAGE

Only pay the lowest possible rate necessary. This advice is repeated so often in the press and on websites that I am reluctant to spend too much time or space repeating it again here. So if you haven't done it already, do it now.

The gist is that unless you're currently tied into a mortgage and it would cost you money to get out, you could probably save yourself a lot of money every month by shopping around for a cheaper mortgage.

How?

Most weekend papers print lists of the 'best deal' mortgages available. Otherwise try websites like:

- ○ www.moneyfacts.co.uk
- ○ www.mortgagesorter.co.uk
- ○ www.yourmortgage.co.uk
- ○ www.moneysupermarket.com

Always check that you're getting the best deal every few years, or as soon as a fixed-rate deal has ended.

74 PAY OFF YOUR MORTGAGE AS QUICKLY AS YOU CAN

I have also heard a very convincing argument for why you should never pay off your mortgage (it is a very cheap way of borrowing money so any spare cash you have you should invest for a higher rate of return than you're borrowing for instead), but even the financial advisor recommending it admitted that he didn't follow his own advice.

So, pay off we shall. Every £10,000 you borrow at, say, 5% interest will cost you £12,500 in interest over a 25-year mortgage. It therefore goes without saying that the more you pay off in the early days, the bigger the savings you will make over the long run.

And if that isn't argument enough (or the right kind of argument for however it is that your mind works), imagine when the time comes when you don't have to pay out a single penny in mortgage. Because you already own your property outright. It belongs to you – not the building society who is happy to let you pretend that you own it, for the sake of the however many thousands of pounds you pay them for the privilege every year.

FURNITURE AND DECOR

Spending on things for your home could be one of the biggest drains on your money. Women in particular will spend an enormous amount of money on the home if they can while still failing to see how they are being profligate. They will go without buying new pants or bras because they don't think they can afford it, but then see building a conservatory or having new wardrobes fitted as an unavoidable necessity.

75 DON'T BORROW MONEY

Only have work done or buy things for the home if you can afford to pay for it now. Don't borrow money to have a new kitchen fitted or buy a £2,000 sofa. Save up until you have the cash to pay for it.

76 OLD THINGS ARE GENERALLY CHEAPER AND BETTER QUALITY

On the whole, buying things like antique chairs or cute retro sixties vases is a lot cheaper than you might expect. Check out the local antique shops before making your way to expensive designer furniture stores. You'll get something truly unique and beautiful.

77 SHOP AT IKEA

I have now read enough articles by interior designers who say they bought their kitchens at Ikea to realise that you'd be dumb not to at least look into doing the same.

78 VISIT FRANCE

French beds and chandeliers for £50 a pop. *Instead of paying high prices for French antiques, why not drive over there yourself and get them for as little as 20% of the price*– and a weekend away in France into the bargain? All you need to do is hire a van, drive to the ferry port then head for the markets.

- Lyon has a great market called the Brocante Stalingrad every Saturday.
- Paris has the market at Port de Vanves every weekend and Marché aux Puces at St. Ouen.
- In Lille, you can visit the famous Lille Braderie car-boot sale during the first weekend of September or the Wazemmes every Sunday morning.

Antique mirrors and frames, ironwork beds, chandeliers, beautiful linen tablecloths, wardrobes and chairs. For a few hundred pounds you could load your lorry full of fantastic bargains. And if you could arrange to sell some of your finds on – to local antique shops or on eBay, for example – you could even make money out of the journey!

79 READ THE CLASSIFIED ADS

People often sell such things as washing machines or dishwashers, for example, if they are moving home and won't need them at the new place. You could save yourself a fortune by taking them off their hands. You could also find that new desk, kitchen table or wardrobe you're looking for at a quarter of the price you'd pay new.

80 JUST ASK

Let your friends, family, work colleagues and others know that you're moving and ask whether they have any spare furniture. The chances are that people will have items that they no longer need and you may even be helping them by getting rid of old furniture cluttering their space.

81 THE JOY OF SKIPS

Discover the joy of looking in skips. A load of discarded Victorian red bricks, for example, could be used to build a beautiful new wall in your garden. Old timber could be reclaimed to make wonderful floorboards for your bathroom. You can even find perfectly good items of furniture, such as old chairs that can be reupholstered or painted. If you find something you want, just remember that you are legally obliged to seek permission from the previous owner before you take it (easier than heading down the road at four in the morning with a torch and a balaclava).

2) RENOVATE KITCHEN UNITS

Don't like your existing kitchen units? Before you take out a huge loan to replace the lot, see if you could completely transform them by painting them and changing the handles. You can even buy special paint specifically for this job. Alternatively, you can just buy new doors instead of replacing the whole units.

3) GET CHEAPER CURTAINS

Curtains can be very expensive. Adverts in local papers can be an excellent source of great bargains, as can charity shops. You can also check out the website www.thecurtainexchange.net.

4) DISCOUNT FURNITURE

This tip is a double-edged sword. In a couple of places around the country, there are warehouses that sell the unsold homeware from each season of brands such as House of Fraser, Laura Ashley and Marks and Spencer:

○ One is near Stansted. Called You're Furnished (01279 815028), it sells furniture, kitchens and bathrooms, etc., at up to 60% cheaper than the high street.

○ Trade Secret is near Oxford (01295 810100). There is also a branch in Sydenham (020 86506131).
○ The Showhome Warehouse is in Northants (01933 411695).

Only ever go to these places if you really have to buy a new sofa, bath or chest of drawers. Do not allow yourself to leave with anything other than a sofa, bath or chest of drawers if you see what I'm telling you.

85 DO IT YOURSELF

There is enormous satisfaction to be had from doing a job yourself. Whether it's as simple as painting a wall or building a new extension, you will save yourself a lot of money by not bringing in the experts. Taking a few days off work to get the job done will also make a very refreshing break from the nine-to-five grind and give you a step outside your everyday life for a few days.

A friend of ours, for example, was quoted several thousand pounds to rebuild a lean-to at the back of his house. He took two days off work instead and did the job himself. The first day was spent staring at the existing construction and then searching through B&Q until he'd found the things he needed for the job. The second day was spent doing the work, drinking mugs of tea and getting to know the trees in his garden and the next-door neighbour.

86 LEARN A FEW PLUMBING BASICS

If you haven't got one already, request a DIY manual as a birthday or Christmas present. Knowing how to deal with a blocked sink or fused kettle could save you a fortune in plumbing bills and by not replacing appliances that just need a bit of fixing.

87) INTERIOR BEAUTY ON A LOW BUDGET

Aim to decorate your house with more careful and personal input rather than just throwing money at it. A room full of thousands of pounds worth of expensive furniture may not be as beautiful as a room where the owners have had time to add their own personal touches and feeling to the decor. A room with plain white walls, wooden chairs and a table rescued from a skip may look more beautiful than a room full of designer furniture. A delicate £20 antique vase with bluebells hand-picked from the garden will give a very different effect than an expensive vase with a pre-made bouquet in it.

88) FLOWERS

Instead of big bunches, look to put just a couple of well-chosen flowers in a well-chosen vase. Either buy just a small selection of individual flowers from a florist or take a pre-made bouquet and divide it up into different vases to put in different rooms in the house.

89) ART

Buy art from local artists. It can be much more satisfying than buying an expensive print for the same price. A great way of getting some real art – and a great way of supporting people who are doing what they really want to do with their lives.

11

PERSONAL FINANCES AND SAVINGS

One of the most bizarre traits of human nature is the sheer number of people who suffer from a complete breakdown of intelligence when it comes to their finances. Even really bright people who earn good wages often seem to come under the influence of some kind of commonsense-disabling drug when it comes to their finances. The impact it can have on both their overall financial and mental health can be absolutely devastating.

I have met people who spend constantly on a credit card and pay several hundred pounds a month on credit card interest, yet actually have enough money coming into their bank accounts to mean that they should never have to buy anything on credit at all. I have talked to other people who are paying monthly sums into savings accounts paying 5% interest a year – yet struggling to pay credit card bills or loans that are ratcheting up interest at the rate of 5% a month. And then, of course, there are the people who just don't seem to be able to keep hold of money no matter how much they have coming in. *So where do you begin if you want to get smarter with your money?*

You start with the first in the list of tips below, then work your way down as many of them as are relevant for your needs and for as long as you can bear it. They are listed in order of importance, at least to ensure you don't miss the important ones at the beginning. In fact, the few at the beginning may take a bit of practice to get the hang of because they go against the grain of everything the financial services industry spends millions every year trying to train you to believe. But I promise you that if you follow these rules – along with some of the extra tips that follow – you will never ever be short of money again. You may also have enough money to live on when you retire.

(90) DON'T BORROW MONEY

Apart from your mortgage, never ever (or almost ever) borrow a single penny of money. And that includes loans, remortgaging, buying anything now but paying for it later and yes, even putting your wonderful new purchase from Selfridges on your credit card *or having an overdraft.*

Now, I know this will sound harsh, and you may even get that financial stupidity kicking in and saying "But how will I be able to afford to pay for anything?". . . but bear with me for a minute.

For starters, let's look at that statement of complaint: "But how will I be able to afford to pay for anything?" A lot of people truly and honestly do believe that they wouldn't be able to afford to buy things if they weren't able to buy them on credit or on credit cards. Yet this is absolute nonsense.

Buying things on credit costs more than buying them outright. Borrow now and you'll be paying more in the future. Pay more in the future and you'll have so many outgoings already that you'll end up having to pay for your groceries on credit. It's a vicious circle that can make even wealthy people feel completely penniless unnecessarily.

91 DON'T EVEN DIP YOUR TOE IN THE RED

One of my least favourite things about driving is when the petrol gauge in my car starts dipping into the red. I immediately become filled with anxiety and desperately need to have that wonderful feeling of a full tank of petrol again.

Many people choose to run their finances with the needle constantly so far into the red that the light is forever flashing and they live in a constant state of mild panic.

They are constantly overdrawn. Constantly paying credit card bills. Constantly stressed about not having enough money. Yet all they need to do to get out of this situation is to make one major shift with their finances – just once – and the whole cycle will be changed once and for all.

All they have to do is fill up the tank with petrol and make sure that it stays full. Clear all their debts and then stay in the black. It may mean a couple of months of going without and catching up, but in a few months' time, you'll be able to breathe easier, feel happier and actually feel much better off.

92 CUT UP CREDIT CARDS

Only ever pay for things by cash or debit card. Spit at those evil loan letters that tell you how you can afford a new car or holiday for just £50 a month, and get some financial order into your life.

Do you realise what you're up against? Using a credit card can be like trying to drive a combine harvester without any tuition or even an instruction manual. The offers and rules can be so complicated that you can very quickly end up paying £100 in avoidable interest payments and fees if you're not meticulous about your finances. Miss a payment, for example (and credit card statements do have a habit of getting lost in the post), and you could not only get stung by a late payment fee, but also lose the right to the low interest rate you were promised when you signed up. They are dangerous things; avoid them at all cost whenever you are able to.

93 SET A WEEKLY BUDGET – AND STICK TO IT

Following on from the previous tip, limit withdrawals to once a week and take out a lump of cash to last the week. Put your cards away and leave for emergency spending only. If you only have the cash in your wallet to spend, you will learn how to use it wisely.

94 GET RID OF FINANCIAL DISORDER IN YOUR LIFE

Having any kind of mess or clutter in your life can make you feel stressed, disorganised and generally a bit peeved. And financial disorder is probably the number one culprit.

But isn't trying to sort it out going to take forever and be more hassle than it's worth?

Well, actually, no. Finding time to transfer money to different credit cards or switching your mortgage may seem like a chore too far for the week, but it really, really, really is worth it.

Whatever it takes to get yourself motivated, make sure you do it. Buy yourself a spanking brand-new hardback notepad or smart shiny box file with a new packet of multicoloured tabbed dividers. Take a half day off work. Enlist the help of a money-minded friend or relative, or visit a bookshop and pick up a few relevant books. Have a good hard look at all the different kinds of debt, savings and investments you may have. Have a look at where you stand with all your bank accounts.

Your aim is to have complete and beautiful financial order, to feel completely in control of your finances. And remember, you should always have the long-term aim of being completely in the black as quickly as possible.

95) KEEP A DIARY

It's a good idea to do this every day, but even if you do it for one week or a month, keeping a note of everything you purchase will help you realise how easily your money can disappear. Once you become conscious about spending a fiver at the coffee shop on the way to work every morning, it might just encourage you to get up a little earlier and make your own breakfast instead.

96) REGULARLY CHECK INTEREST RATES

Make sure that you are paying the lowest possible interest rate on every penny you owe. Pay off store cards and anything with a higher interest rate immediately. Consolidate your loans and borrowings in one place with the lowest possible rate. Take advantage of new credit card offers where you can transfer your existing balance and pay 0% interest on your borrowings for six months. In fact, if you are paying a single penny in interest on any kind of borrowing, then you are paying too much.

(97) *CONSIDER A 'LIFE OF BALANCE' TRANSFER*

If you are trying to pay off your debts with as low a rate as possible, the obvious answer is to keep switching every few months to cards offering 0% for transfers. If you are not brilliant at disciplined and dedicated management of your finances, however, this may not be the best option for you. What may well be the better answer is what is known as a 'life of balance' transfer. With these offers you pay only a very low rate (currently around 5%) which lasts until you have paid off every penny of the balance transferred. It may not be 0% but it may well work out a lot cheaper for you in the long run.

(98) *GET RID OF ALL YOUR DEBTS AND GET BACK IN THE BLACK*

If this means living on baked bean curry and pasta with tomato sauce for a month, then so be it. Extend the tidy-up to the rest of the house and sell unwanted belongings at a car boot sale or on eBay. Make sure you call in all money that may be owing to you (expenses not claimed at work, money lent to a friend), and take back that unwanted Christmas present for a refund.

(99) *AN EXTRA JOB TO HELP YOU OUT*

If you're in a bit of a financial hole, you could even consider a part- time job for a short while to get you back in the black and feeling rich again. A bit of night-time taxi driving could give you the extra space you need to think your life out.

100 DON'T BE A FINANCIAL OSTRICH

You already know who you are if you do it. Never ignore or stop reading bank or credit card statements because you don't want to know what they say. Never ignore a mounting amount of debts or even summons. Don't try to fool yourself that most people run their lives by getting further and further into debt. Don't try to fool yourself that you're still too young and irresponsible to worry about such boring things as money. Don't believe that one day it will all magically sort itself out.

101 AVOID GAMBLING

Don't waste money on lotteries, gambling or investments that are so speculative as to be practically throwing money down the drain. According to Richard Dale in 'The First Crash', both gambling and get-rich-quick schemes were immensely popular among all classes of society in the early 18th century. In 1700, however, average life expectancy was probably under 20. If you weren't killed off by smallpox, typhoid, typhus, dysentery or tuberculosis, you'd probably be killed in battle, in child birth or by your local robber or highwayman.

"The brevity and uncertainty of early eighteenth century life no doubt shaped people's attitude to money. A career committed to the laborious acquisition of wealth over time was perhaps less appealing than taking a chance on some get-rich-quick commercial venture."

Whereas for those of us in the 21st century, who are probably going to be around well into our eighties, "labourious acquisition of wealth" is unfortunately more along the lines of where we need to be heading.

(102) CLAIM EVERY FORM OF BENEFIT FROM THE GOVERNMENT THAT YOU ARE ENTITLED TO

If you are made redundant, for example, don't be too proud to claim unemployment benefit immediately.

Every single child, no matter how wealthy the parents, is entitled to Child Benefit. Claim Child Tax Credit if your joint wage has been below £50,000 – even if it's just for one year.

Most over 65 are underclaiming. *If you're over 65 then there's a very good chance that you're not claiming enough.* According to the BBC, as many as 50% of people with disabilities and long-term health conditions tend to under claim on Disability Living Allowance (for under 65) and Attendance Allowance (for over 65). People of pension age tend to vastly under claim on Pension Credit, Housing Benefit and Council Tax Benefit.

(103) OPEN A SAVINGS ACCOUNT

Have problems building up savings? Open up a savings account with a high rate of return, and then set up a direct debit payment into it from your current account. Make sure this comes out a day or two after you get your salary and I swear you will hardly miss it. In fact, it will give you a helping hand in curbing your overspending. If you see that you have spare cash in your account, you will probably spend it. If you don't see it, you won't spend so much. Saving accounts where you pay in a set monthly amount generally also pay higher rates than almost any other kind of account.

04 DITCH THE PERSONAL PENSION

There are better ways of planning for your retirement. Who knows what the rules will be by the time you retire, but there's a good chance that – particularly if you're on a lowish to medium income – every penny of the money you put into a personal pension will have been wasted. Or rather, you won't get any more money after all your years of saving than other non-savers will get from the government. With state pensions increasingly means-tested, it may actually make better financial sense not to save into a pension plan but to use other ways of saving instead.

And are private pensions really such a good idea anyway? A recent survey by Moneyfacts showed that one in four pension funds have lost money over the past ten years. It is only the tax relief you receive on your contributions that prevents you from actually losing more money than you put in. Another fact to consider is that, with a personal pension plan, you may get the tax rebated at the front end when you put the money in, but you will be taxed at the other end on all the retirement money you receive.

05 ALTERNATIVES TO TAKING OUT A PERSONAL PENSION

Well, the world's really your oyster. You could invest the money yourself for hopefully far higher returns and look for ways of paying less or no tax on the returns that you get. More and more people look to property as a way of paying for their retirement. Or you could simply start accumulating nice things that (hopefully) won't depreciate in value – such as art, antiques and jewellery – and then plan to sell them off whenever you need the money!

OPT FOR A SIPP

SIPPs (self-invested personal pensions) are becoming more and more popular – despite the fact that you will not be allowed to hold residential property in them as was previously planned.

Basically, they are just like ordinary personal pensions. For example, you still get to benefit from the 22 or 40% tax rebate you get from the government when you pay into your pension – only you decide where your money is invested. You can invest in anything from individual shares to unit trusts, overseas stock markets, commercial property and gold bullion. If you run your own company, you could even hold your office in your SIPP.

All you need to do to set one up is visit the website of one of the low-cost providers such as:

○ Hargreaves Lansdown (www.hargreaveslansdown.co.uk)
○ Sippdeal (www.sippdeal.co.uk)
○ Alliance Trust (www.alliancetrust.com)

These will administer your SIPP for as little as £80 per year. All you have to do then is decide where to put your money.

Any UK resident can contribute up to £3,600 a year into a SIPP, even if they have no taxable earnings. The maximum amount you may contribute to your pension (as of 2006–07) is £215,000!

SIPPs are generally recommended for people who want to pay a relatively larger amount into their pension – or people who have already built up a significant pension fund. For a SIPP to be worth considering, you probably need to have £25,000 or more in, or available for, your pension fund – or be able to pay in £1,000 or more a month.

107 IF YOU'RE RETIRED – LOOK AT GARS

Already retired? How could you be getting a 40% higher income from your annuity than you are today?

"Hundreds of thousands of investors approaching retirement should check whether their pensions have a valuable guaranteed annuity rate (Gar) because it could boost their retirement income by thousands of pounds a year."

said an article in *The Sunday Times* recently. 'Gars' provide a retirement income up to 40% higher than a standard annuity, yet many people do not even realise their policy comes with a guarantee. Many insurance companies will fail to point this opportunity out to you, so it is up to you to check whether you have this option. Some Gars can pay as much as 10% a year – compared with the roughly 6% now being offered by the average annuity.

PLAN TO WORK FOR LONGER!

In 1950, an average male would have retired at 67 and expected to live for another 11 years. Today, with the average life expectancy for a man at 84 and expected to rise even further, wouldn't it make sense that the retirement age should come a little later? In fact, the average person these days can expect to work until they're 63 – many spending much of their working day dreaming of ways of making it come sooner.

But will your retirement years be all the fun and games you expect of them? Especially if you somehow have to support yourself for another 21 years after you stop working.

Of course, not everybody will be able to work until they're 80, but here's a thought that's worth considering: Rather than working the next 20 years in a job that you don't really like because it will enable you to retire early… would it not be better to plan to work for the next 30 years, but only making money in a way that gives you a great deal of satisfaction? After all, there are only so many Sudoku puzzles you can do before you start wishing you had a job to go to and colleagues to talk to.

GET A JOB WITH THE GOVERNMENT

It used to be that taking a job in the public sector meant a lower earning potential than that in the private sector. Not so any more. Between spring and summer 2005, average hourly wages (paid out of your taxes) rose 23p to £11.79. In the private sector, meantime, hourly wages fell 5p to £10.17. If you work in the public sector, you are also provided with a pension, and you're also pretty certain to be able to start drawing your pension a few years earlier as well.

10) ONLY INVEST IN WHAT YOU UNDERSTAND

A lot of the investments that private investors make are too random or inappropriate. In fact, if you follow no other rule when it comes to investing then follow this: buy or invest only in what you really know and understand. Too many people invest willy-nilly in hunches, impulses or tips or adverts they read or hear about. They don't really know whether the stock is right for them, whether it should be short- or long-term or how it should sit in a portfolio of investments.

11) GET FINANCIAL ADVICE FOR FREE

If you're buying something like a unit trust or life insurance product directly from the company, be aware that you're actually paying them the commission that an Independent Financial Advisor (IFA) could have received if you'd bought it through them. Most IFAs will not actually charge you anything for their advice but will make their money by receiving this commission. Unless you're 100% sure you know which product is best for you, it may well be worth going to an IFA for advice first. Do bear in mind, however, that some IFAs will lean towards recommending those products that will pay them the most commission.

112 ARE YOU PAYING TOO MUCH FOR LIFE INSURANCE?

If you bought a life insurance policy without shopping around (when you took out your mortgage, for example), chances are you could save a considerable amount each year by moving to a new one now.

113 THE CHEAPEST AND SIMPLEST WAY TO BUY GOLD

The most cost-effective, safe and simple way of buying, owning, storing and selling gold, starting from just one gram up, is at BullionVault.com. There you can buy gold bullion at live market prices, which is then stored for you – in your name – in a Brinks vault in Zurich. You will pay no more than 80p in transaction costs for every £100 you invest. The best you can do with coin dealerships, banks or most gold dealers, on the other hand, is pay at least 4% over the market price. Then you've got to fork out for storage and insurance on top, as well as losing another 4% (or more) off the market value when you come to sell.

114 INVESTIGATE WAYS TO SAVE TAX

Most people who are able to put some money aside should consider taking out a tax-efficient Individual Savings Account (ISA). You can use an ISA to save up to £3,000 a year in cash – or invest up to £7,000 a year in shares. You will not have to pay any personal income or capital gains tax on either the income or capital gain.

You can also invest up to £25 each month with a Friendly Society tax-exempt savings plan for a minimum of ten years. This can be on top or instead of your ISA allowance.

115) DON'T GIVE ADULT CHILDREN TOO MUCH MONEY

Research shows that adults who are used to having their life subsidised by their parents are more likely to be spenders rather than savers.

116) PAY 0% INSTEAD OF 40% TAX

If you're a higher rate taxpayer then avoid paying 40% tax on savings, or 32.5% on dividends, by putting them in your partner's name if they are a basic rate taxpayer or maybe even pay no tax at all. That way you can pay just 20% tax or none at all. Also bear in mind that if only one partner is a higher rate taxpayer, you may be better off putting money into their personal pension only – thus getting a 40% refund from the government. If you are a non-taxpayer, talk to your building society about having interest paid gross.

117) CHECK IF YOU'RE PAYING THE RIGHT TAX

Many people are overcharged. Make sure you are not being overcharged by checking your tax code. Refer to leaflet P3, 'Understanding Your Tax Code', available on the HM Revenue & Customs website, and ask questions about anything you don't understand. Many people, for example, continue to be charged for benefits they are no longer receiving.

MAKE SURE YOU HAVE WRITTEN A WILL

If you don't have a will, it is not guaranteed that all your wealth will be passed on to your loved ones – even if it's your spouse or children. It needn't be anything fancy; you can simply buy a ready-to-write will from a stationery shop and fill it in yourself.

12

HOUSEHOLD EXPENSES

○ Cut your gas, electricity and phone bills by as much as 30% instantly – and save the planet as well
○ Save thousands of pounds on health care, dentists, care homes, council tax, insurance and even death

GAS AND ELECTRICITY

The average home spends £500–600 a year on its gas and electricity bills, and I don't know about you but I know that my home and family have never been average. For many years I actually got enjoyment out of leaving lights on around the house – in retaliation, I believe, for being constantly told off for leaving lights on as a kid. Today I get a mental image of pennies dropping into a wonderful big piggy bank every time I turn a light off, unplug the telly or cut my potatoes into smaller chunks to reduce the time they will need boiling.

The message here, therefore, is to try to cut down on your fuel consumption without having to compromise your aesthetic preferences, your enjoyment of life and your right to be warm.

SWITCH GAS AND ELECTRICITY SUPPLIER NOW

The exact amount varies depending on where you read it, but it is estimated that the average person can save somewhere between £100 and £250 a year just by switching their gas and electricity suppliers. All you need to do is visit one of the new utility switching websites, enter a few details and then take a meter reading. No need to change pipes or wires or have a man in a boiler suit spend half an hour in your airing cupboard. And yes, you can even do it over the phone as well.

Here are contact details for some of the companies that do it:

○ www.saveonyourbills.co.uk (Tel: 0845 123 5278)
○ www.uswitch.com (Tel: 0800 404 7908)
○ www.energyhelpline.com (Tel: 0800 074 0745)

Some of these companies will even offer you a cash back incentive if they can help you switch. For the most up-to-date information on switching, visit Martin Lewis' website, www. moneysavingexpert.com.

 SWITCH TO DIRECT DEBIT

Save £187 – switch to DD. A recent report from Bacs Payment Schemes – the company which operates direct debit in the UK – claims each household could save an estimated £187 per year if they paid by direct debit (for utility bills, health insurance, breakdown cover and satellite TV). The biggest savings, it says, are to be had on gas and electricity bills.

1) REPLACE AN OLD BOILER

Changing an old boiler to a high-efficiency condensing boiler can save you as much as 30% on your bills.

2) TURN DOWN THE THERMOSTAT

Already done that? Then how about turning the heat down by 10°C to save as much as 10%, 20°C to save 20% on your heating bills – and enjoy wearing those thermal vests, warm socks and cardigans. A comfortable working environment is about 19°C.

3) MOVE YOUR FURNITURE AROUND

Put your bed next to an internal rather than an external wall to keep toasty in bed. Avoid putting any furniture in front of radiators to allow for maximum heat.

4) GOOD HEAVY CURTAINS

Draughty windows can be very expensive when it comes to heating bills. If you're not a fan of double glazing (and some point out that the cost of installing it will never be covered by the savings you make on heating bills, even over a lifetime), then make sure you have good heavy curtains. If that's too costly, you could look around for a decent pair in charity shops – dyed in the washing machine if you don't like the colour. And, on the subject of curtains, don't forget to draw them as soon as the sun goes down to keep in the heat.

125 DRAUGHT-PROOFING

Alternatively, ask at your local DIY shop about your best options for low-cost draught-proofing.

126 GET FREE MONEY TO IMPROVE THE ENERGY SAVINGS IN YOUR HOME

Find out whether you're eligible for free grants to improve the energy-saving measures in your home. Some are even available through energy suppliers who are forced by the government to do their bit when it comes to improving domestic energy efficiency and tackling global warming. Visit the Energy Saving Trust website at www.est.org.uk (Tel: 0800 512 012) and fill in their form to see whether you can benefit. Those over 60 will certainly be eligible for lots of freebies.

127 ALWAYS TURN OFF THE POWER SWITCH

Leaving appliances like TVs and videos on standby is actually when they use a vast proportion of their energy. Eighty-five per cent of the energy used by a DVD is wasted when it's not in use. Only 5% of the energy used by mobile phone chargers is used to charge phones – the rest is used when you leave it plugged in at the wall without a phone attached to it.

128 HALVE THE COST OF FREEZERS

Keep the freezer full – even if you bulk out with scrunched-up paper. It uses less electricity per pound of food and less electricity overall.

29) RETHINK YOUR WASHING MACHINE CYCLES

Wash with fuller loads in the washing machine and remember that the higher the temperature, the more money it will cost you. A 40°C wash will save you up to three quarters of the cost of the hottest cycle!

30) USE SUNSHINE

Getting out in the sun is not only one of the best ways to get a happiness and health boost, it's also great for your energy bills as well. There's no better smell in the world than line-dried washing, so get out in the garden and hang out the washing – instead of wasting £5–8 a week on drying it in the tumble dryer. Also use sun streaming through windows to heat rooms and remember to open connecting doors to let the heat travel round the house.

31) EMBRACE THE COLD OUTDOORS

On a beautiful crisp winter's day, turn off the heating and set off for a long walk in the countryside instead of moping around the house wasting money on heating.

32) TO TUMBLE DRY OR NOT TO TUMBLE DRY?

Drying on a line or clothes horse is obviously the best option but not always possible. I have been unable to find conclusive information about whether it is more economical and green to dry clothes on radiators or put them through the tumble dryer. Friends of the Earth, however, do say that using the radiator increases your fuel use by stopping heat reaching the room.

It can also create damp and encourage the growth of mould. If you do use a tumble dryer, make sure clothes are really well spun before you start to dry them. Another alternative is to hang clothes on a dryer in a room and open the windows.

(133) THERE'S ALWAYS MORE YOU CAN DO

Apparently there are still homes without any loft insulation and naughty people who don't lag their hot water tanks, put lids on boiling saucepans or turn the lights off when they leave the room.

Your parents were right. Lights do use around 10–15% of your electricity bill.

(134) GOOD NEWS FOR BATH LOVERS

It may not be the case that a shower is cheaper than a bath – due to a lot of people having power showers, the source of the hot water or energy, and whether you just use it to get clean or to escape from the kids or the in-laws for an extra ten minutes. I have also found that I can do some of my most important work of the day during 15 minutes spent in the bath. Brilliant ideas had in the shower disappear much more easily than those had in the bath.

(135) MOVE TO A SMALLER HOME

Of course, a lot of money on heating and fossil fuel consumption can be saved if you move to a smaller, newer home built with the previous tips in mind, but that's a step too far in my books. But not, perhaps, for some.

WATER

36 *A BOTTLE IN THE CISTERN*

Fill a plastic bottle with stones and slot it into a space in the cistern of your toilet. This can save many litres a day being wasted every time you flush it.

37 *NEVER LEAVE A TAP RUNNING*

Many of us would probably plead guilty to leaving the tap running whilst brushing our teeth. To break the habit, start using a beaker. Likewise, when washing up, fill a washing-up bowl or the sink rather than trying to 'wash and go' under a running tap.

38 *WAIT FOR A FULL LOAD*

Fill up your dishwasher and washing machine as much as possible (without overloading, of course!) before switching them on. As well as wasting electricity caused by unnecessary extra cycles, less water will be used in a fuller load than a half load.

TELEPHONES

39 *HAVE NO PHONE AT ALL*

When I was growing up, we never had our own phone line in our house. We had an extension line set up from my grand-mother's house next door and did very well out of it.

I doubt whether many of the readers of this book would realistically want to go without a phone altogether, but it is an option worth considering.

One person I know survives without a phone at home but relies heavily on emails to friends to arrange his social life, etc. He is lucky enough to have a phone box near his home and pops out to make calls when necessary. I believe he then uses the phone at work to chat to his mother ...

(140) USE YOUR PC AS YOUR PHONE

Another completely free way to make calls if you have an internet connection (especially if you have broadband) is to make calls from PC to PC. Both you and the people you call will need a PC (obviously), a microphone, a headset/speakers and the software which is now available for free from companies like Skype (www.skype.com). It takes very little time to set up and could certainly save you a lot of money, especially if you regularly call overseas.

(141) HALVE THE COST OF YOUR HOME PHONELINE

The first thing I'd like to confess to you here is that I cannot give you the answer to what are the definite cheapest ways to run a home phone line. I have spent hours puzzling over the impenetrable maze of my BT phone bill and months wondering whether it was cheaper to use two different companies, three different companies or just go back to using BT alone.

The truth, in fact, is that there are so many differences in pricing (cheap land calls but expensive to mobiles, cheap to Orange but expensive to O2, cheap off-peak package but expensive during the day, etc.) that even those who call themselves experts in this matter confess that it is almost impossible to say what is the best option, even when you know a person's individual usage habits.

42 GET SOME ADVICE

My best piece of advice is to take yourself to the website of the money saving expert Martin Lewis (www.moneysavingexpert. com). Or, to save you even more time still, I have condensed the very best advice I believe he (currently) has to offer into three easy steps. (Remember, of course, that offers are changing constantly, so it always pays to update yourself on the latest options every six months):

1. Use BT as your basic line rental; but you must make sure you're on their most basic, 'Option 1' tariff.
2. You then use the CPS provider, Just-Dial Saver (www.just-dial. com) to get free phone calls for the evenings and weekends.
3. Finally, for calls to mobiles and landlines during the day use 1899.com (www.call1899.co.uk). All you have to do is sign up to Just-Dial Saver as your main provider and open an account with 1899.com. For evening and weekend calls you only have to dial the number normally. For calls to mobiles and landlines during the day, simply remember to dial 1899 before the number.

43 SAVE AS MUCH AS 90% ON INTERNATIONAL CALLS

For international calls my mother put me on to 1st Phonecards (www.1stPhoneCards.co.uk, Tel: 0845 123 5858). Simply check out the different options available on the destinations you regularly phone. Cards cost as little as £5, with calls from 1p a minute or less. They will email you a prepaid phonecard with instructions on how to call.

(144) DON'T BE EMBARRASSED TO WAIT TILL AFTER 6

Why not wait until after 6 o'clock to call and get your phone calls for free – or practically for free. Being careful with your money is fashionable these days.

(145) KEEP PHONE CALLS TO MOBILES SHORT

The no. 1 place for savings. Remind yourself – and everyone else in your household – to keep phone calls to mobiles as short as possible. 50p a minute really can add up to a small fortune.

(146) KEEP AN EYE OPEN FOR NEW OFFERS

Remember that there is huge competition in the world of telecommunications and that things will therefore change very quickly. Every year, or even every six months, check to make sure that you're not missing out on much cheaper options. Visit www.moneysavingexpert.com whenever you feel like saving a bit more!

MOBILE PHONES

(147) DO YOU REALLY NEED IT?

And even if you do need it, but only for emergencies and maybe one or two calls a week, you shouldn't be paying any more than £5 a month to do so.

Simply be more aware of the savings that are available. When I told a friend recently that I was writing a book about saving money, she was very eager to know what she could do herself because she was pretty certain that she was already being as thrifty as possible.

"Take mobile phones, for example," I started lecturing, "so many people are on monthly payment plans costing them £25 or more a month when they could easily be spending more like a fiver a month by using a cheaper tariff, company or Pay As You Go option."

"I am!" she quickly confessed. "And I only really have it in case I break down with the kids in the car! I never use it."

Which is further proof of the fact that we could all save so much more if we only realise exactly where it is that we can cut corners, spend less or save. And don't forget, £25 a month is £300 a year! It really is worth making the effort and spending half an hour of your time to find a cheaper option.

48) SWITCH AND SAVE HUNDREDS OF POUNDS A YEAR

If you're on a monthly contract, then you're probably paying for the right to have a new phone every year. If you don't need a new phone every year, then you're paying too much and could save a lot by changing contract. You can get out of any contract if you've been in it for over a year and there are now a number of companies that will allow you to transfer your existing number and phone and cut your phone bills by £10, £20, even £30 a month. I found www.easymobile.com a very nice, straightforward site to use.

(149) *ADVANCED SAVINGS*

Visit the Onecompare website (www.onecompare.com) to find
out which switching options would work out the cheapest for
you. Spending some time making sure you have the right tariff or
Pay As You Go deal for your personal usage could save you a fortune. Changing your usage habits could also save you hundreds
of pounds a year.

(150) *MAKE FEWER AND SHORTER CALLS*

Many people these days use their mobile phones all the time
simply because they can. If you're a heavy user, cut your calls in
half and you could have several hundred pounds more a year to
spend on other things you'd like to buy. Being able to call people constantly is also a bit of an addiction, which psychologists
are beginning to recognise as unhealthy.

(151) *AVOID THE BIG NAME COMPANIES*

Buying your phone or tariff from the big companies – especially Carphone Warehouse, The Link and Phones4u – will
almost certainly turn out a lot more expensive than if you buy
from a smaller firm.

(152) *CHEAPER OPTIONS WHEN USING YOUR MOBILE FROM OVERSEAS*

It can be a very satisfying novelty and luxury to pick up your
mobile and make a call when you're overseas. It does, however, cost a fortune. Even sending a text message will cost you
between 35p and 49p (although receiving them is free). The

cheapest option is to buy a prepaid local phone card at your destination (from newsagents or tobacconists) and phone from a landline. You could even buy a card before you go from 1st Phonecards (www.1stphonecards.co.uk, Tel: 0845 123 5858). Calls from the States or Australia, for example, will cost about 3p per minute if you phone from a landline with a card.

If you still want to use your mobile for convenience, the cheapest way to do it is to buy a local PAYG sim card when you arrive on holiday. You will see them advertised at airports, railway stations and other tourist destinations. All you then need to do is temporarily swap the new sim card for the one you currently have in your phone.

3. PHONE PEOPLE AT HOME

Also remember that just because you're phoning from a mobile, it doesn't mean you have to phone people on their mobile. Make sure you have everybody's home number in your phone. Keep calls as short as possible and only phone when necessary.

INTERNET CONNECTIONS

4. DO YOU REALLY NEED IT?

For most people, having an internet connection at home is a luxury. Figures from the Office for National Statistics show that 85% of households with gross income over £1,085 per month have access to the internet at home – compared with just 12% of households with income below £123 a week. If you can afford to pay for it and enjoy the luxury then that's fine. Do remember, however, that if you're paying £25 a month then that's £300 a year. If you're looking to cut down on your outgoings, then this is one possibility.

(155) ACCESS THE INTERNET FOR FREE

You can access the internet for free at almost all public libraries. Libraries also smell nice and are a fantastic place to people watch, get free books and videos, and enjoy a wonderfully electric form of peace and quiet.

(156) MONTHLY DEALS ARE NOT ALWAYS THE BEST

A monthly package may not be the cheapest option. My father is very careful about how much time he spends online and spends no more than £5 a month on phone calls.

(157) CHEAPEST OPTIONS FOR BOTH DIALUP AND BROADBAND

If you've been using the same option for some time, you could easily save £100 a year or more by shopping around and switching – every year or so. Once again, www.moneysavingexpert.com is probably your best first port of call for the very latest top bargains and cheapest options.

(158) WAIT FOR A CHEAPER DEAL

One thing to bear in mind, however, is that with competition getting fiercer and technology advancing at the lightning speed it does, it will probably always be possible to get yourself a cheaper deal in a few months' time. So don't allow yourself to get too wound up about it. Don't feel guilty if you're stuck in a year-long contract and paying more than you think you should be. Don't let it bother you if a friend starts boasting about how little they're paying. These things are going to get cheaper and cheaper, so chances are that once you've finished the contract you're in now, you'll be able to pick up an amazingly cheap deal in ten months' time!

59) *ADDICTED TO SHOPPING ONLINE?*

Another thing to bear in mind is that having immediate access to the internet at home can be a real danger for people who like to shop online. Although we saw earlier in the shopping section how not going to the shops is one of the best ways to spend a lot less money, if you have access to online shops then it could be the equivalent to giving an alcoholic a job in an off-licence.

60) *GET FREEBIES ONLINE*

Visit the site www.freebielist.com where you can claim hundreds of things for free including free product samples, free games, free postcards and free electronic reminder services. Alternatively, why not replace shopping with a hobby known as 'comping'? Visit the website www.prizefinder.com and from there you can enter hundreds of competitions to win cash, holidays, electrical goods, books and more.

61) *SAVE MONEY ON HOME COMPUTERS*

Many people are very good at fooling themselves that they 'need' a new computer when in fact the case is that they really, really, really just want one. Next time you want to upgrade to a new computer, check whether it is really necessary – whether you really need that £1,500 model. If a new computer isn't an absolute necessity now, delay the purchase by six months or a year. Reducing the number of times you update all electronic equipment like this can save you a fortune over your lifetime – and it's good for the environment. Also remember that you don't need the most beautiful computer available to do what you want to do. If you want it and can afford it, then good for you.

INSURANCE

(162) SHOP AROUND

I obviously don't need to tell you that the best way to pay less for your car, home or holiday insurance is to shop around. But don't just continue with the same insurer that was the cheapest last year. You will probably be able to find a better deal elsewhere.

(163) CHEAPER CAR INSURANCE FOR LOW USERS

For car insurance, do remember to tell your insurer if you drive less than 12,000 miles a year, or if you don't use your car to drive to work.

(164) WEBSITES THAT HUNT FOR BARGAINS ARE NOT ALWAYS THE BEST OPTION

Don't be fooled by websites offering to help you find the cheapest deals available. While you may certainly be able to get good deals using this route, I have found that ringing a local insurance broker can bring in even more competitive quotes.

65 *CUT CAR INSURANCE COST BY AROUND 5% BY ELIMINATING THE COURTESY CAR OPTION*

It may sound like a nice treat but will you really need a hire car if it ever happens that your car is off the road for repairs for a few days? Also bear in mind that if you have 'uninsured loss protection' and an accident is not your fault, you can reclaim the cost of car hire from the third party.

66 *BUILDINGS INSURANCE*

When buying buildings insurance, the premium you have to pay can be worked out by either a bedroom-rated policy or a sum-insured policy. Which comes in cheaper for you will depend on what kind of home you live in. Get quotes for both types.

COUNCIL TAX

Fed up with paying over £1,000 a month for your council tax but not really feeling that you get any benefit out of it? Here are a few ways of reducing the amount you pay – or increasing the value of what you get back for what you pay.

67 *GET THE MOST OUT OF THE FACILITIES YOU'RE PAYING FOR*

Council tax goes towards paying for schools, roads, libraries, leisure facilities such as swimming pools, the police and fire brigade, rubbish collection, adult learning, parks and open spaces, galleries and museums, cemeteries and a few other things. Therefore, if you're paying for a private school, buying your own books or building your own roads, then you really are paying double.

Go out of your way to use the facilities provided by your council and you could gain in many ways. For example, ring your county council, ask to be put through to the Adult Education Centre and request a prospectus for the courses that they run. In my own area I can study everything from one-off courses on chocolate making, the Italian Renaissance and buying a home in France, to 15-week career courses in counselling or management, or bookbinding, clock repair, tai chi, stained glass or plumbing.

(168) MANY PEOPLE OVER 60 DON'T CLAIM THEIR REDUCTIONS

According to the organisation Help The Aged, *up to one and three quarter million people over 60 could get help with their council tax but aren't currently claiming it.* A single person aged over 65 with an income of less than £131.95 a week can get all their council tax paid. A couple can get all their council tax paid if their joint weekly income is £197.65 a week or less. For people aged 60–64, these amounts are £114.05 a week for a single person or £174.05 a week between them for a couple.

Carers can get all their council tax paid even if their income is £26.35 a week more than these amounts. People who are severely disabled can get all their council tax paid even if their income is £46.75 a week higher.

If your income is higher than these amounts you may still get some of your council tax paid. And if your council tax is more than the average, you may still get some help even if you have a higher income than shown here. It is always worth checking.

69 IS YOUR HOME IN THE WRONG BAND?

You may be able to lower the amount of council tax you pay if you can persuade the council to change the valuation band of the property you live in. Every property is placed in one of eight valuation bands, A to H. Get in touch with your local council and ask how you can go about appealing against your valuation.

OTHER

70 GET FEWER HAIRCUTS, PERMS AND COLOUR

Increase the gap between haircuts by just one or two weeks and save money over the long term. Opt for haircuts that don't need redoing so often and save a fortune. A friend of mine got so fed up with spending £40 a month on haircuts that he shaved it all off and looks years younger for it.

71 GET FREE HAIRCUTS

For cuts, colour and perms for free or very little, look out for hair salons advertising for models. You don't have to look like a model to be a model for a hairdresser and the work is always supervised, so very little risk is involved.

72 PAY LESS FOR DENTISTS AND ALTERNATIVE AND PRIVATE HEALTH CARE

If you're planning to have a child in the next year, you could get a £330 payout for just £264 put in, plus your dental and optical bills paid (up to £160 and £140, respectively), and 80%

paid of the cost of any homeopathy, acupuncture, hospital consultations, health screening and more. In fact, for most people, they are likely to get a lot more back than they pay in, especially if they wear contact lenses.

How is this possible? Instead of forking out for private health care – and then private dental bills on top – opt instead for one of the cash plans organised by companies such as:

○ HSA (www.hsa.co.uk, Tel: 0800 072 6712)
○ Westfield Health (www.westfieldhealth.com, Tel: 0845 602 1629)
○ Foresters Cash4Health (www.foresters.co.uk, Tel: 08457 990011)

Save money on care home bills. Move to Scotland where the government pays your fees.

173 DON'T BUY YOUR CONTACT LENSES FROM AN OPTICIAN

If you have an up-to-date prescription, then you can easily save around 40% by buying lenses online. I was very satisfied with the customer service provided by the company www.contactlenses.co.uk and would recommend them for speed and ease as well. One tip I would give is that if you are short-sighted and therefore a negative prescription (e.g. -2.50), make sure you order these rather than the positive and therefore long-sighted prescription as I did on my first visit!

174 BUY INK CARTRIDGES ONLINE

If you buy your printer ink cartridges from a high street shop, then you're probably paying way above the odds. Far cheaper options are available online at websites such as www.inkfactory .com. If you receive an advertising flyer with a magazine or newspaper, make sure you shop around before taking them up on their offer. Sometimes, those who trumpet the best deals don't actually have them.

175) *PROTECT YOURSELF FROM BURGLARY*

Even if you have insurance, being burgled is never fun and will probably end up costing you money one way or another. My local policeman told me that most theft crimes are opportunistic – thieves always choosing the targets that offer the easiest entry and least resistance. In fact, a large percentage of thefts happen during the day in summer where burglars simply climb through open windows.

Make sure you have good locks on your doors – and windows too, if possible. Lock your garden shed. Never leave windows open if you are going out.

If you live in an area where there are car thefts, invest in a wheel lock. You will probably have seen on telly that thieves can break into them in minutes, but that two minutes of hassle and potential danger may be enough to make them move on to the next car.

176) *PAY LESS FOR YOUR DIVORCE*

The average UK divorce now costs £750 in solicitor's fees alone. It is, however, possible to cut the lawyers out completely. You will need to find the nearest county court that deals with divorce and collect a form D8 from them – as well as a D8A if you have children. You will then have to sit down with your spouse and fill them out. Once completed, return to the court with the £180 fee. Be sure to include three copies of the D8 form. The judge will then review your papers. It is essential that you are in agreement, especially about what will happen to the children.

13

FOOD AND DRINK

○ Rediscovering the pleasure of muddy potatoes
○ Why real food will make you feel better, live better and spend a lot less money
○ How to spend no more than £20 when you go to the supermarket

During a visit to my elderly grandparents, my very kind and smiling grandmother presented me with a scented candle in a ceramic pot with the words 'domestic virtue' – the meaning of my name apparently – written on it. Rather than be filled with feminist rage at the suggestion, I actually found myself feeling very proud of it. 'Domestic virtue' is something I think we should all aspire to – because we have already gone so far down the other routes of domestic sin, domestic slovenliness or domestic indifference that we need to recover a bit of harmony. For many people, cooking meals has become a chore that they'd rather not be bothered with, preferring instead to spend the time watching television. Most of us will grumble if we have to do as much as wash our own salad leaves or peel a potato.

£20 billion of food is thrown away each year – five times more than we spend on aid.

Yet what could be a better way to unwind at the end of the day than to spend 20 minutes in the garden picking home-grown herbs and tomatoes – a glass of wine in hand in the style of Floyd if you fancy? What better pleasure than the smell of chopped lemon thyme, the joy of a big muddy parsnip or watching a home-baked loaf of bread coming out of the oven.

Really getting in touch with our food and our eating is the perfect antidote to this technology-driven, fast-paced and somewhat plastic life that we lead these days. Indeed, one of the major factors that creates our general grumpiness and dissatisfaction with life is the fact that we expect so much from it – instead of realising that real happiness comes when you take real pleasure in everyday activities like sharpening knives, oiling locks or neatly folding jumpers into a pleasantly scented drawer.

And then, of course, there is the expense of food. One thing all of my friends agree on is that it's very difficult to cut down on how much you spend on food (and wine, of course). You may be able to survive another season in a bra that used to be a bikini top, but you still manage to spend £130 every time you set foot in Sainsbury's.

So for those of you whose financial black hole is nothing more glamorous than having a big hungry family and a penchant for nice food to eat, here are some tips for saving money on food while improving the quality of your life.

77) *BUY FRESH PRODUCTS FROM MARKETS*

Buy fresh food from markets, butchers and local greengrocers instead of supermarkets as it will be a lot cheaper. We all talk about the delights of shopping at markets in foreign countries, yet markets in the UK can be just as exciting and fulfilling.

78) *BUY EXACTLY WHAT YOU NEED AND NO MORE*

If you need three mushrooms to make a meal extra tasty, then buy just three mushrooms. If you need one leek, buy one leek. If you need two rashers of bacon then ask for just two at the butchers.

79) *EAT BETTER TO FEEL BRIGHTER, HAPPIER AND LESS ANGRY*

The papers have been full of Jamie Oliver stories about why our kids should eat better – but how about us? In a story in the papers in May 2005, Icknield High School in Luton reported that its GCSE exam results had improved massively since it had hired a good chef to make healthy meals. The head also reported that the children seemed so much happier and well-behaved. Brighter, happier and less angry? There are a lot of adults who could do with some of that as well! Cut down on junk and convenience foods as much as possible and concentrate on buying fresh produce – for you as well as the kids.

80) *PLAN BEFORE YOU SHOP*

Rather than heading off to the supermarket in search of some food for the week, sit down first and actually plan what meals you are going to cook and what ingredients you will need.

(181) *DON'T SHOP ON AN EMPTY STOMACH*

If you go to the supermarket hungry, you are more likely to pick up that quick snack for the journey home and buy things that you suddenly crave once you see them. Even if you pop in on the way home from work to pick up something for dinner, you'll be tempted to buy 'extras' to go with your meal that you probably won't be hungry for later.

(182) *BEWARE OF '2 FOR 1'*

Once you're in the supermarket, stick to what's on your shopping list. If you see brilliant '2 for 1' bargains that are too good to miss, think carefully first about whether it will really save you money. However, it can be a particularly useful way to stock up on goods that you regularly buy.

(183) *EAT LESS EXPENSIVE MEALS*

You also need to plan meals that are generally economical – rather than the ones that require three different kinds of fish, a packet of shallots and some weird Indonesian ingredient that you will never ever use again. Keep a list of the meals that are cheap to cook but pleasing to you and pin the recipes up in the kitchen. Macaroni cheese (with a bit of bacon), bean soup with garlic bread, egg and chips (chips from the fish and chip shop), toad in the hole and pasta with nothing more than olive oil, parmesan and black pepper are all favourites with my family, for example.

84) GO FOR CHEAPER CUTS OF MEAT

Become aware of which are the cheaper meats to cook with, and cook with them creatively. Chicken livers, for example, are cheap and make some quite spectacular meals including chicken liver pate. Pork steaks are cheaper than beef steaks. Cheaper cuts of meat (stewing steak, for example) are often tastier than the more expensive cuts – because you need to cook them in tasty stews for longer lengths of time to tenderise them.

85) GET INSPIRATION FROM COOKBOOKS

We all have them but how often do we use them? Spend a whole evening flicking through cookbooks and making a list of recipes you'd like to try – especially ones that won't cost too much to make. You could even photocopy each of the recipes you fancy to try and make it easier to get round to using them. Do miss out ingredients that are more expensive if you think the meal will still be just as good without them.

'Changing the Way You Shop, Cook and Eat' – is the sub-title of a cookery book I've been reading called 'The New English Kitchen' by Rose Prince. The main message of the book is that if you buy good (and even what some would call expensive) ingredients, you can still spend less on food overall and yet also shop more conscientiously – by choosing wisely, cooking yourself and making really delicious food go further. In the section on bread, for example, she says:

"Bread can pull off a feat that few cooked foods are capable of: as it matures, it develops new and interesting uses. In other

words, it ages gracefully. Once past its sandwich era, older bread fits easily into simple recipes: it lies beneath radiant vegetable broths, turns up in a bread, red wine and onion soup, blends smoothly into a clove-infused sauce, and can be sweetly saturated by a creamy, eggy custard with spices and fruit. There's always toast, too, an edible plate for favourite things. The bread that can do this is not sliced and wrapped, sometimes costing little more than a first-class stamp, but made in the slower tradition. This bread has real integrity but it costs a bit more – which is why it is worth knowing how to use it for ages."

She gives recipes for breadcrumbs as well – including breadcrumb and garlic with pasta and a Sicilian breadcrumb salad.

Other tips from this book that I particularly like include:

○ You can buy a whole wild rabbit for £3 from the butchers and feed four.
○ Scampi and langoustine are actually the same thing. They are expensive to buy fresh but the shells toasted in a pan and then boiled in water make a lovely broth.
○ Good tinned tuna can be a culinary delight and better than an overcooked piece of the expensive fresh fish – good for fish cakes or added to semi-soft boiled eggs and lettuce hearts, for example.
○ A whole cooked ham will keep in the fridge for ten days and has endless uses that mean you won't get bored of it.

- Veal calves are actually a necessary by-product of milk production (i.e. the boy cows that don't make milk) so if you buy British veal (not crated European) you are actually doing cows a favour.
- Roast a large piece of beef and serve cold as a great way of feeding a large number of people – with lime and sesame dressing on rice thread noodles or with a watercress and winter sauce (mayonnaise, chicken stock, Tobasco sauce, Worcestershire sauce, S + P and mustard).

36) MAKE MORE EXPENSIVE INGREDIENTS GO FURTHER

Use the same ingredient (creatively) for a couple of meals in a row. My husband makes a tasty pasta dish, for example, using onions, garlic, bacon, chicken livers, a few tomatoes and a handful of spinach. The rest of the packet of spinach can be used to make a potato, spinach and chickpea curry the following day. If you buy a tub of herbs for one dish, make sure you get the most out of it by adding it to, or planning, a few other meals around it as well.

37) LOTS OF TASTE FOR PENNIES

Spices, bacon and a pot of single cream are all good ingredients for making food a lot tastier and classier with not a lot of expense. A tub of dried chilli powder and a packet of cumin seeds can make delicious meals for less than 1p at a time – especially if you make sure you keep on using them.

188 THINK BACK TO STUDENT DAYS

Dig out your old student cookbook or pick one up in a charity shop for 50p. This will give you lots of great ideas for saving money and lots of recipes for tasty cheap meals.

189 EAT YOUR CUPBOARD DOWN

If you've got the kind of kitchen cupboard that's full of half-used packets of lentils and forgotten tins of produce then have a week where you use up everything that's been sitting around in there. At the end of the experiment you get the enjoyment of a tidy, clean cupboard and you'll probably have saved yourself at least £5 on meals for the week.

190 FREEZE HALF OF THE MEAL

When you cook food like curries, soups or a Bolognese sauce, make sure you freeze half of it to be used for a meal on another day. I have found that if I allow my family to eat as much of it as we like before the remains go in the freezer then there won't be any remains, so divide it up first. Deliberately making big batches and freezing portions can also save a lot of energy and time spent cooking in the long run. Having some home-cooked meals in the freezer will allow you to have a fast meal without having to resort to ready-made meals.

191 HOME-MADE SOUP ONLY TAKES 20 MINUTES TO PREPARE

Remember that as long as you have onions and chicken stock cubes in the house, you can make a tasty soup out of practically anything. Serve with home-made bread and you'll make even the biggest food lover happy!

2) BUY FOODS WHEN THEY ARE IN SEASON AS THEY WILL BE TASTIER AND CHEAPER

In the UK, for example, leeks are in season from September to April, apples and pears from September to October, broccoli from February to May, cabbage in the winter, lettuce in the summer and tomatoes from August to October.

3) USE YOUR GARDEN

Grow herbs, fruit and vegetables in your garden and you could save yourself a lot of money and discover why the smell of soil really can lift your soul. With a variety of free herbs at your disposal, rustling up tasty meals on a budget can become much easier. Add your freshly grown basil to pasta with butter, garlic and chilli. Serve anything with a sprinkle of delicious parsley to instantly transform it. And even expensive foods like rocket and cherry tomatoes are very easy to grow.

Don't know where or how to start? How about a trip to a local nursery or garden centre. They're great places for a day out and you can very quickly get an idea of what you can start doing by just browsing around or asking for advice.

> Sow parsley seeds in spring in the ground or in containers.

Rosemary and grey-green garden thyme are both hardy plants that are easy to grow but which also look attractive in the garden. Salad rocket is self-seeding and can be harvested almost all year round. Sow from late winter all the way through to autumn.

Plant tomato plants in early June in growing bags, fertile soil, pots or even in a hanging basket if you opt for the bush variety.

Ask for a fruit tree as a Christmas present.

(194) DON'T HAVE A GARDEN?

Herbs can easily be grown in pots on a windowsill, tomatoes in a bag on a doorstep. Or how about getting yourself some gardening space in an allotment near your home? If you ever hanker after some therapeutic peace and quiet and a bit of space of your own then this could also be a solution to what your body, heart and soul have been yearning for. Human beings need contact with nature to stay sane and happy. Imagine the tranquillity of walking across the dewy dawn grass with the birds singing and flitting in the bushes, the smell of moist soil on your wellington boots as you bend down to give a firm tug on the tough green stalk to pull up your own home-grown brussels sprouts or potatoes.

Ring your local council and ask to be put through to someone who can give you information about allotments. You can also get more information from the National Society of Allotment and Leisure Gardeners, O'Dell House, Hunters Road, Corby, Northants NN17 5JE. Tel: 01536 266. Fax: 01536 264509. Email: natsoc@nsalg.org.uk. Website: www .nsalg.org.uk.

55) MAKE MONEY FROM YOUR GARDEN

If you grow a good batch of, say, organic herbs, you could also make money on the side by selling them to a local organic produce store.

56) SAVE £1,000 ON LUNCHES

> "If you normally spend £4 a day on takeaway lunches you could save around £1,000 each year if you make your own lunch."

'Save Cash and Save the Planet', Andrea Smith and Nicola Baird.

57) SPEND A LOT OF MONEY ON WINE?

Then set yourself the target of spending at least £1 less per bottle. Look out for offers at supermarkets and wine shops. Take the car for a weekend in France and double up the holiday as a booze trip.

58) DON'T OVERSPEND ON DINNER GUESTS

If you're trying to live on a tighter budget, then don't spend too much money on making meals for people when they come round for dinner. The most jubilant responses I've ever got from dinner guests was by serving them a really good shepherd's pie or a roast dinner with crisp roast potatoes, roast parsnips and yorkshire puddings.

MAKE YOUR OWN JAMS, BREADS AND PICKLES

I can't guarantee it will save you loads of money but it will bring you a lot of satisfaction. Making a batch of jam or marmalade, pickles or chutneys is a better way of spending an evening than moaning about the lack of good programmes on telly – and the many jars you'll make could last you a whole year. Home-made bread doesn't need to take any more than five minutes to prepare if you have a bread machine, 15 minutes if you have a food mixer and only a little longer if you knead it by hand. The pleasure, however, increases the more time you put into it.

 SAVE £50 TO £100 A YEAR ON PAPER KITCHEN ROLLS

Use J cloths for small spills, drying-up cloths for drying and keep a loo roll handy in the kitchen. Use 'mop up squares' (cut up old towels or T-shirts) for bigger spills and emergencies.

 SPEND LESS WHILE STILL ENJOYING GOOD ORGANIC FOOD

Want to buy organic but find it makes your shopping so much more expensive? I'm not going to go into arguments about why you should (or shouldn't) go organic, or bore you with facts about cancer-causing pesticides. What I have managed to find, however, are a few useful facts and solutions that can help you cut the cost if you would prefer to be organic as far as you can afford it.

○ **Box schemes**
  The Soil Association says that the best way to cut the cost of going organic is to use a box scheme or find local sources. In fact, *"buying organic fruit and veg through a box*

scheme can actually work out cheaper than buying the equivalent non-organic food". On the Why Organic website (www .whyorganic.org) you can find an Organic Directory that will help you find your closest outlet of organic foods including vegetable box schemes, farmers' markets, farm gates and mail order.

○ **Selection**

The more you eat of a food, the more pesticides you will get from it. It might therefore be wise to concentrate mainly on the foods you eat more of – pasta, potatoes and apples, for example.

○ **Peeling**

"Peeling will not remove all residues (particularly systemic pesticides which go more than skin deep) but it is a practical way to reduce them, and is useful advice to consumers, particularly those who cannot afford or do not have access to organic food." (*Pesticides News* No. 56).

○ **Fruit and vegetables**

Which? analysed government tests on samples of fruit and vegetables over the past four years and found persistent problems with pesticide residues in certain produce. It was found that between a third and nearly half of all fruit and vegetable samples contained detectable pesticide residues and up to 3% of these levels were above the legal limit. The main offenders were apples, carrots, celery, lettuce, pears and strawberries.

An article published by *The Independent* newspaper in April 2005 analysed the for and against arguments for a list of different foods, also taking into consideration the differences in price. Some of its interesting conclusions include:

1. 59p instead of 36p on a tin of Heinz organic baked beans is well worth the price – especially as "New research reported in *New Scientist* in January [2005] showed that organic tomato sauce (and ketchup) contains up to three times the normal levels of lycopene".

2. Organic means nothing when applied to white bread and all refined foods. "The outer husks of the grain where the pesticides collect have all been removed along with any pesticidal threat," says Suzannah Olivier, the author of 'Food Medicine'.

3. Organic eggs and milk are worth the extra expense.

4. Organic beef and lamb are not. "All cattle and sheep in the UK have access to grassland and are not intensively reared. . . . Even ideological organic food eaters draw the line at paying extra for organic red meat."

5. "I'd starve rather than buy non-organic chicken," says Joanna Blythman, the author of 'Shopped: The Shocking Power of British Supermarkets'.

(202) DISCOVER THE JOY OF GROWING YOUR OWN SPROUTS

Sprouts like alfalfa, sunflower, clover and soybean are not only one of the most nutritiously intense foods you can eat, they can also be grown cheaply and easily at home, any time of the year and in just one week!

Most dried beans, pulses, lentils and seeds can be sprouted and make a delicious and crunchy addition to salads. Just follow the following instructions:

1. Half fill a container with water, add a couple of teaspoons of the rinsed seeds or pulses and put them in a warm place overnight.
2. Next day, fix a piece of muslin (or clean tights or stockings) over the top of the jar or container with an elastic band. Drain away the water, then rinse, drain again and leave to stand upside down on a draining board or a tray.
3. Repeat the washing a few times a day – always making sure the sprouts are thoroughly drained to avoid rotting. Take out any fuzzy or mouldy looking seeds.
4. After 2–3 days of rinsing and draining, alfalfa, lentil, mung bean, radish and sunflower sprouts will burst through their hulls. (The hulls can either be eaten or removed as preferred.)
5. If sprouting alfalfa, put them on a sunny windowsill once they have grown their first leaves and wait 4–6 days until they have reached about 12 inches in height. Lentils take about 3–4 days to grow and are ready when they have grown about 1/4–1/2 an inch. Mung beans need 3–5 days growing time and have to be kept in a warm, dark place. They are ready when they have reached between 1/2 and 2 inches. Sunflower seeds need about 2–3 days growing time and are ready when they have grown less than 1/2 an inch.

14

UNNECESSARY EXPENDITURE

"Asceticism is not that you should not own anything, but that nothing should own you."

Ali Ibn Abi Talib (656–661)

"A measure of dry bread, head bowed in thanksgiving, water from a pleasant slope, that is all one could ask."

Poem by an 8th-century Christian

A human being can survive happily on very little. I have even been told by a friend that we can survive healthily on a diet of nothing but baked beans!

Drawing the line between what are good and excessive expenses in life is not an easy task – and is one that you need to work on by yourself.

On the one hand, of course, the line can be a very practical one. If you earn a decent salary, for example, yet get stressed out by your overdraft, then some unnecessary or excessive spending is almost certainly going on. The pleasure of earning good money, surely, should be in the comfort it affords – not a cause of discomfort because it is still not enough. Your aim should be to reduce your spending to a level which allows you to feel that you are actually earning *more* than you need. Only then can you begin to feel wealthy and contented.

But what if you earn so much that you are able to afford all kinds of luxury items and purchases? Because that, of course, comes with its own set of problems.

- Remember that only a limited amount of happiness can come from the objects and luxuries that you own.
- Remember that the desire for endless luxuries can show that something is lacking in a person's life, and both stems from and causes emotional problems. Don't be lured into unrequited longing by advertising and magazines or by the desire to impress the people you know and meet with the expensive things you can afford.
- Remember that the less you spend, the less you will have to work to be able to afford it. The less time you spend spending, the more time you can spend living.

Still not sure what counts as excessive or unnecessary spending? Here are a few pointers.

 THE HIGH PRICE YOU PAY FOR LUXURY

Spending ridiculous amounts of money on such things as plates, sheets and duvet covers is surely unnecessary when you can get perfectly beautiful ones much cheaper.

04) QUESTION YOUR DESIRE FOR THE REALLY EXPENSIVE OPTIONS

In fact, any expensive 'luxury' purchases where far cheaper options would have been available should at least be brought into question. Why spend £30,000 on a new kitchen suite, for example, when you can get really gorgeous ones at Ikea? Why spend £50 on a bottle of face cream when a £5 one with less chemicals may actually be better for the long-term health of your skin?

05) DO YOU REALLY NEED THAT?

Watch out for unnecessary 'useful things' you might be lured into getting when buying things for babies, kitchens or your personal entertainment. In my opinion, machines that individually wrap nappies are out, for example, as are spoon rests in the kitchen and any kind of executive toy for grown adults. If you're not sure whether something qualifies for this category, ask yourself whether it would look out of place in the *Innovations* catalogue.

06) PAMPERING

Money spent on any kind of 'pampering' is something you should also be wary of. Spending money on pampering is often either a sign of having nothing better to do with your life or a compensation for how exhausted and stressed out you are by your job. Just imagine how much younger you would look if you only had to work until 5PM instead of 7PM.

WHY DO YOU WANT TO BUY THAT?

For men especially, the buying of expensive but unnecessary items (especially for themselves) is often a symptom of being somehow unhappy in their lives or jobs.

 ## SECOND HOMES

I would also like to put second homes overseas in this category – unless you can honestly say that it works out cheaper than staying in a hotel or renting. 'A good investment' might be an argument but I have serious doubts about how much more of a property boom can be expected in most of the popular destinations.

 ## REPLACING ANYTHING JUST BECAUSE YOU FANCY A NEW ONE IS ALMOST CERTAINLY EXCESSIVE

A super-expensive, super-snazzy coffee machine, for example, may impress some people, others may see it as too showy, excessive or even nouveau riche.

 ## LIVE DOWN TO IMPRESS

In fact, the trend of the moment is definitely more along the lines of bohemian taste rather than eighties decadence. Serving Prosecco is far trendier than champagne. A home-made apple crumble wins points over a tart from a French patisserie. A tatty old fridge may impress your friends more than a brand spanking new one.

11 FIRST CLASS?

Flying first class is surely unnecessary unless you really, really need to.

12 WATCH OUT FOR THOSE ACCESSORIES

Overspending on accessories such as jewellery, bags, shoes, ties and scarves is easy to do – whether it's buying too many and/or spending too much on individual items. If it's a good fake, nobody will know it's not real unless they come over and bite it.

Be wary of overspending on anything. Especially if you can't afford it.

13 DON'T TRY TO KEEP UP WITH THE BECKHAMS

This means paying more for anything than you can really afford in the hope that it will impress your friends, your family or your neighbours.

14 THE DANGER OF DESIRABLE CONSUMABLES

Be aware of the powerful allure of desirable consumables. Avoid, for example, spending £360 on a trendy Eglu chicken house, because you want to live the good life. I am only picking on this as a handy example rather than the epitome of excessiveness. In fact, if you were at all in the market for a chicken house, then this model might seem very beautiful and desirable. But that is exactly the danger of desirable consumables. They project such a powerful aura of niceness, neatness and perfection that we are fooled into believing they will make our lives feel perfect too.

They are luring us away from what is real in life, and it is only in the real that we can really find happiness.

Buy some wood and chicken wire instead. Take joy in the feel of the soft wood giving way to the sharp metal of the nails. Take pride in a job well done. Take pleasure as the wood slowly darkens with the weather and settles into your garden – not pain as the prim plastic of your Eglu house gets covered in chicken poo and stands out in your garden like a sore and expensive thumb.

15

KIDS, SCHOOLS AND UNIVERSITIES

○ The most important gift you can give your children is education
○ The damage caused by too much TV and advertising
○ Numerous ways to cut the cost of having kids – the damage you can do to them!

Our kids have it easy, right? They really have it good.

Yet the more I read about it and the more I think about it, the more I realise that the consumer culture we live in could be doing them a whole load of harm.

And I'm not talking about having 'money' as being bad. Being brought up in a family that has lots of money isn't bad for kids. It's all about how the money is obtained and spent and the value that is given to material considerations and possessions compared to other values in life. In fact, these days a kid being brought up in a poorer family can quite easily be more adversely affected by money obsession and consumerism than kids from a wealthier background.

Money, you see, isn't really the issue here. And neither is love. The problem we are actually facing is one of misdirection, and a failure to really notice what is going on in our world.

The BBC website recently had an article on what it is like to grow up in Africa. I was really struck by what the responders had to say:

"The sheer happiness and contentedness is unimaginable. The African culture of village oneness is foreign in the western culture. In the African village, lack of excessive material greed and amassing excessive wealth trains the African child to be considerate."

Simon, West Palm Beach, USA

"I am now living in the United States of America but nothing compares to my childhood in Nigeria. Africa is a wonderland. It is blessed by God. It is home to some of the world's most creative and kind and talented people. I remember Lagos city nights, getting oranges peeled by fruit vendors in the street. I remember attending Fela Kuti shows with my dad. I remember stories."

Eseohe Arhebamen, New York, USA

"I have great memories of my childhood. From the freedom of running around barefoot to adventures in the bush to climbing trees in a quest for wild fruit and playing house. We lit mini charcoal fires like our mums and spent lazy

afternoons comparing who had the prettiest clay babies . . .
Lovely summer holidays spent at Grandma's house where
20 or so cousins slept on the floor and ate fruit and vegetables
from her garden. I miss the togetherness and laughter
of those days."

Rachel, Zambia

I'm not saying that our children don't enjoy happiness, wonder, togetherness or laughter, I just think we should doublecheck that the material and technological bias of the society we live in doesn't get in the way of other qualities, pastimes and values.

The tips in this book are all about how spending less money on your kids can be better for everyone.

KIDS

215 GIVE THEM THE IMPORTANT THINGS IN LIFE

Don't give your kids an electronic car that costs £200 and will barely be played with after the first three days. Give them love of others. Give them the ability to be content. Teach them how to find joy and wonder in the small details of life.

216 TEACH THEM AWE AND WONDER

For example, on a dewy morning, head outside armed with a black piece of sugar paper and go looking for cobwebs. Impressive cobweb found, push the paper right up against it so that the dewy wetness makes a perfect copy of the web on the paper. Next, take a piece of chalk and trace over all the lines to make a perfect representation of the cobweb once the water has evaporated.

It is the ability to take pleasure in the everyday beauty of the world and life that will set your children up for lifelong happiness.

217 AN EASY FORMULA FOR BETTER PARENTING?

Nowhere is the 'Spend Less, Live Better' mantra actually more important than when it comes to bringing up your kids. Not only will they bleed you of every penny you have if you spend too much on them, but doing so could actually considerably damage their personalities and lives as well. Relentless consumption leads to a dissatisfaction with life. An obsession with the material and the advantages that money can buy can lead to a paucity in the spiritual and a forgetting of the advantages that can be given to a kid for free.

If you can aim to give your kids the best life you can with more personal effort and thought and less material possessions or expense, there's a very good chance you'll be heading in the right direction. Spending money is always going to be the easy option with kids, but a reliance on consumer goods and easy answers or pleasures is not the way to give your kids the gift of lifelong contentedness and happiness.

218 THE JOY OF SIMPLE PLAY

Conventional play is undeniably being replaced by television and video games. Think back to your own childhood and your own happiest memories of play. For me it is playing hide-and-seek with a group of cousins who lived nearby, making perfume water with rose petals and feeding mud pies to our dog. We had our own special gang and even wrote a handbook where we listed details of all our gang's rules, weapons and strategies for defence.

> Today we have kids who spend more time consuming than they spend actually playing.

219 MATERIALISM AND CONSUMERISM AS A CAUSE OF DISSATISFACTION AND DEPRESSION

If exposure to an excess of advertising, shopping and continual retail temptation is bad for us adults, then spare a thought for what it's doing to our kids.

Kids these days are far more exposed to the pervasive powers of advertising and branding than we ever were when we were young. The industries themselves have also become much more irresponsible and powerful.

In her book, 'Born to Buy: The Commercialised Child and the New Consumer Culture', Juliet B. Schor tells us that:

"A 2001 Nickelodeon study found that the average ten year old has memorised 300 to 400 brands. Among eight to fourteen year olds, 92 percent of requests are brand specific."

The number one aspiration that children have these days is to be rich – a far more appealing prospect apparently than being a great athlete, a celebrity or being really clever. And remember, the general aim of advertising is to make the viewer or reader feel that without the product advertised either they or their life is somehow wanting or inadequate.

Ms Schor tells us that amongst marketing professionals there is even an acronym which describes how the retail and advertising industries are constantly trying to target younger kids with products that were designed for much older children. KAGOY stands for Kids Are Getting Older Younger.

Also note that it was the advertisers who originally co-opted the hip-hop look of African-American street culture into their ads – bringing the famous hoody to the streets of Britain and making violence, drugs and criminality something for our kids to aspire to.

No wonder then that the conclusion Juliet B. Schor comes to in her book is that:

"Involvement in consumer culture causes dysfunction in the forms of depression, anxiety, low self-esteem, and psychosomatic complaints."

The more kids want, the unhappier they become.

"Encouraging age-inappropriate behaviour and desires can create confusion and erode genuine self-esteem."

The more they rely on the excitement, surprise and bright colours of television and consumer packaging, the less equipped they will be to appreciate the real values of life or the beauty of a simple acorn.

220) BEWARE OF 'I WANT, I WANT, I WANT'

However good a parent you are and however well you have brought up your kids, there will always come a time when they start asking if they can have things. The urge to possess and hoard seems to be a basic human instinct. Shops and marketers have also become very good at doing their jobs. Here are a few ideas to help you deal with the 'I want, I want, I want' urges in your children. You will also be doing them a massive favour if you can teach them to rein in this instinct now rather than take it with them into adulthood.

221) DON'T BUY YOUR CHILDREN THINGS WHEN YOU'RE OUT

If they want something that they see, resist the urge to say yes even though you can afford it. They have to learn that they can't have everything they see that vaguely tickles their fancy and if you teach them that they can then you're on a very slippery slope to bankruptcy – either real or emotional.

222) TAKE YOUR CHILDREN TO LIBRARIES

With my first daughter I would often go to bookshops with her and got into the habit of buying her a book almost every time we went. Books are a personal consumer weakness of my own and I think I justified it as teaching her a love of books. I soon realised, however, that what I was actually doing was teaching her a love of buying. Today we go to bookshops only occasionally and rarely leave with anything more than a slightly suspicious eyeing from the shop assistant.

223 GIVE YOUR CHILDREN AN ALLOWANCE

Set a weekly allowance and let them decide how to spend it.

224 SPEND LESS TIME IN SHOPS WITH THEM

If you don't go shopping with them, you won't be put in a position to buy something for them to keep them quiet and happy.

225 EXPLAIN WHY HAVING TOO MANY THINGS IS NOT VERY GOOD

For younger children this may be as simple as repeating phrases like "Oh, you don't need any more of those", or "If you have too many things, none of them will be special". It is amazing how the right vocabulary can change your child's whole outlook. For older children you might try explaining to them about fossil fuels or actually take them to a landfill site.

226 FIND THEM ROLE MODELS OF AUSTERITY

From books, stories or history. The autobiography of dancer Isadora Duncan, for example, would be great for older girls. Younger girls can be given a slightly adapted take on Cinderella (the ugly sisters are horrible and ugly because they think more about things than people and animals).

227 IT ALL STARTS WITH YOU

Remember that the way children learn how to be in life is by mimicking their parents' behaviour. If they see you shop all the time then they'll grow up wanting to shop all the time themselves. If daddy seems happiest when he buys himself a new toy, little Johnny will aspire to the joy of a continual supply of new things too.

The best way to ensure your kids grow into the adults you'd like them to be is by becoming a role model for that lifestyle and personality yourself.

8) CHILDREN NEED TO BE AT ONE WITH NATURE

A connection to the natural world around us is profoundly important for the health and happiness of human beings. Indeed, much of the isolation, loneliness and lack of meaning many people feel as adults partly stems from the dislocation they suffer in a world that has become one long dash from the office to the car to the home to the television. Help children to develop a love of nature now and you will be giving them a gift for life.

As Edith Cobb wrote in 'The Ecology of Imagination in Childhood':

"The study of the child in nature, culture and society reveals that there is a special period, the little–understood, prepubertal, halcyon middle age of childhood, approximately from five or six to eleven or twelve – between the strivings of animal infancy and the storms of adolescence – when the natural world is experienced in some highly evocative way, producing in the child a sense of some profound continuity with natural processes and presenting overt evidence of a biological basis of intuition."

GIVE YOUR CHILDREN REAL NATURE EXPERIENCES

Don't leave the responsibility to school trips and outings. Take them out yourself on walks down muddy paths or go for an adventure in the marshes. As Alan Dyer and John Hodgson say in their book, 'Let Your Children Go Back to Nature', it is not enough for children to experience nature as detached observers with clipboards, cagoules and questionnaires. *They need to sit around a fire at twilight, being told stories of tree spirits and dragons*; build nests, dens, tree houses or tunnels; dress up in costumes and play games in forests. The aim is to:

> *"re-enchant our land in the imagination of children: to give young Adventurers the opportunity to enter the magical and perilous worlds of Nature, Landscape and Myth, and to become transformed by the experience."*

 ONLY BUY TOYS YOUR CHILDREN WILL PLAY WITH

Between 1995 and 2000 alone, the number of toys sold annually rose by 20%. Yet can you honestly say that your children really play with even 20% of the toys that have been bought for them? Get to know what's going on in the toy market and whether your child would actually enjoy and want to play with the latest fad rather than buying it because all their friends have it.

 BORROW TOYS

Borrow them from toy libraries in your area (contact the National Association of Toy and Leisure Libraries for contacts in your area on 020 7255 4600). Make an arrangement with friends whereby you have regular toy swaps.

2) CHEAP WAYS TO BUY TOYS

Make a real effort not to buy too many, or buy them from charity shops and give them a good wash. You can often find gems of unwanted toys hidden in car boot sales. Teach the children how to make toys for themselves.

3) DON'T OVERSPEND AT CHRISTMAS

When buying for your kids try to remember how excited they are by the first ten presents they open, but how the law of diminishing returns seems to make them really quite jaded to the experience shortly after that. Instead of just buying them things you see at random, set a maximum budget for each child before you start and don't be tempted to go beyond it.

And don't spend too much on children under two!

Children love the spectacle, the fun and the sheer magic of Christmas, so concentrate on giving them that.

4) NAPPIES, BABYGROWS, BABY WIPES AND MORE

Using reusable nappies instead of disposables will save you between £400 and £500 – more if your second child uses the same set of nappies, which mine very happily has. Financial savings, however, are only part of the story.

Ignore government-backed studies that tell you that disposable and reusable both use the same amount of fossil fuels, as these are based on the reusable user tumble-drying every wash. Neither do they take into account that up to *7 million trees are cut down to produce nappies for UK babies each and every year*, that we create one million tonnes of nappy waste each year or that this waste will take anywhere from 200 to 500 years to decompose.

Still not convinced?

Then how about the fact that the super absorber (sodium polyacrylate) that makes disposables so absorbent was removed from tampons in 1985 because of its links with toxic shock syndrome (TSS). The chemical has also been found to be lethal if inhaled by cats. Research carried out in Germany suggests that disposable nappies may have an adverse affect on the development of a boy's reproductive system. A study from America published in October 1999 linked disposable nappies to asthma.

Baby wipes also contain chemicals that aren't all that nice.

Try using more natural varieties or just a bit of recycled loo roll dipped in a bit of water.

(235) USE CHILDCARE VOUCHERS

Parents with children under the age of 15 can make use of childcare vouchers. They can be used for nurseries, playgroups, childminders and au pairs who are registered by Ofsted. Most large companies run childcare voucher schemes, but if yours doesn't, it's always worth asking them to consider it as it shouldn't cost them any money.

6 PUT SOME REAL EFFORT INTO HELPING YOUR KIDS BECOME LEARNERS

There are a lot of great books around to help good parents like us become even better parents and our children to become bright and happy people. Bill Lucas and Alistair Smith's 'Help Your Child To Succeed', for example, gives useful tips like:

○ Some children can be reluctant to learn if they feel that learning is too risky because there's always quite a high likelihood of failing. Try to give your child a feeling of safety by letting them know it's OK to make mistakes. Always give four positive comments for any negative one.

○ Help them develop a strong sense of self-worth and identity by encouraging them to talk about their feelings. This is especially important in boys who tend not to express themselves so freely.

○ Spending time with your children is one of the most important gifts you can give them. Try to have some time when you remove all disruptions and concentrate exclusively on your child. You might read a book together, visit a play area or fix a bicycle. This 'together time' is when you can shape attitudes and develop the kind of positive habits that encourage learning.

37 START EARLY

About half of a person's learning ability develops by the age of four and 80% by the age of eight.

SCHOOLS

 238 DON'T DRIVE THEM TO SCHOOL EVERY DAY

Doing the school run twice a day isn't just bad for the environment as well as the quickest way of eating up a tank of petrol, it also denies your children the chance to take more exercise, clear their heads on the way to school, chat with friends in a relaxed environment and take in the many wonders of the changing seasons and the natural world as they walk to school.

239 ORGANISE A WALKING GROUP

If you live within a half-hour walk from school, organise a walking bus group so that a group of kids can do the walk together, accompanied by different adults on different days.

240 WHEN DRIVING SEEMS LIKE THE ONLY OPTION

If you live too far to walk, is there another solution? Could you change schools? Cycle with them to school? Or at least try and organise a lift share with other parents.

241 STATE SCHOOL, PRIVATE SCHOOL OR HOUSE IN THE RIGHT CATCHMENT AREA?

I am not going to give an opinion here about whether I believe private schools to be right or wrong morally and politically. What this book does believe, however, is that unless sending your kid to private school is easily within your financial means then doing so may well be unnecessary. In fact, if doing so means that both parents need to work full-time to afford it then there's also the possibility that you could actually be doing the kids more harm than good.

2) WHY A LOCAL STATE SCHOOL CAN BE BETTER THAN A PRIVATE SCHOOL

As long as the local state school isn't a bad one, your children will probably perform pretty much as well there as they would at a good private one. The fact that the average private school child gets higher grades than the average child at state school may initially make you think that the education they receive is far superior. Think about it a bit deeper, however, and you'll realise that it's not that simple. In fact, the superior performance of the children can be seen to have far more to do with the kind of children they are due to the kind of parents they have, than the actual schooling. After all, if you send your children to private school it's because you really value the importance of education. And that one fact alone will probably do more to influence your child's school performance than any other factor.

3) YOU ARE MORE IMPORTANT THAN THE SCHOOL YOUR CHILDREN GO TO

People are obsessed about getting the right schools for their children. It is an acknowledged fact, however, that a far more important factor for your children's success (and happiness) in life is having the right parents. There are better ways of being a good parent for your child than putting them through private education. Perhaps it is better to downshift your lifestyle aspirations than to have both parents working full-time during the children's early years. Perhaps it would be better for dad to be at home for the kids on an evening than for him to be able to afford to buy them everything. *Perhaps it is more important that the parents have the time and energy to talk to their children* about the wonders of science, architecture or jelly fish than for them to learn to speak in a posh accent.

If your kids are bright and they get the right guidance from you then they will do brilliantly regardless of the school they go to.

 MAKING SURE THEY GET A GOOD PLACE AT UNIVERSITY AND ARE COMFORTABLE THERE

Another important thing to bear in mind is that the leading universities will take a child's schooling into consideration when deciding whether or not to make them an offer and with what grades. They realise that if a child can perform very well at a middling school then they are probably quite a bit brighter than a child hitting the same kind of grades at a top private. So that £20,000 a year on education may not in fact have been money well spent.

Also note that boys who attend the most expensive schools are the most likely students to under-perform at university. A study of almost 50,000 students by academics at Warwick University found that a pupil attending a £20,000-a-year school had a 15% lower chance of obtaining a good degree than other undergraduates with the same A-level results.

15) WANT THEM TO HAVE A POSH ACCENT AND UNDERSTANDING OF THE CLASSICS?

Send them for elocution lessons and inspire them with an interest in Helen of Troy yourself.

16) BAD SCHOOLS IN YOUR AREA?

Take the plunge and move to somewhere the schools are better.

47) DON'T JUST RELY ON SCHOOL PERFORMANCE OR LEAGUE TABLES

While they are obviously a very good indication, it is always worth visiting the school and asking questions as well. Even a school with a below national average figure might still have 20% of students at the top getting very good marks.

48) OVER 100,000 FAMILIES ALREADY SCHOOL THEIR CHILDREN AT HOME

You have a legal right to opt to teach your children yourself, taking as much or as little as you want from the National Curriculum. It is a particularly beneficial choice for bright children who are not responding well to the school experience or who do not seem to be getting on there. It is also worth noting that home-schooled children do actually tend to outperform their peers at school – a reason, perhaps, why 30% of those parents choosing this option are teachers themselves.

For more help and information on home educating, visit Home Education Advisory Service (http://www.heas.org.uk) or Education Otherwise (www.education-otherwise.org).

UNIVERSITY

 249 DECISIONS ABOUT UNIVERSITY

When making decisions about university, bear in mind the cost – in time, money and missed opportunities. With Britain the third most expensive country to study in (after New Zealand and Japan), according to the Global Higher Education Rankings report, it makes sense for both you and your children to try and reduce the cost wherever possible. A recent NatWest Bank report showed that students now leave university with an average debt of more than £12,000 and can easily spend a decade paying it off.

Do your children really want to go, and is it the best option for them? With such a large percentage of school leavers going on to university these days, it no longer necessarily gives them the advantage it used to. Would they be better opting for an apprenticeship in carpentry or organic gardening? Is a media studies degree really going to get them that job at the BBC they think it will?

250 UNIVERSITIES THAT HELP WITH COSTS

Which universities offer their own grants and bursaries? When choosing a college it is worth bearing in mind that some offer their own maintenance grants and bursaries in addition to those offered by the government. This could make a significant difference to the cost of living.

51) CHEAPER ACCOMMODATION

Another important thing to bear in mind is the cost of accommodation at the different universities where your children may wish to study. Students at Salford, Cardiff and Manchester, for example, will pay only half the accommodation costs faced by those studying at the London universities.

52) LIVING IN HALLS OF RESIDENCE

In general, where good accommodation is provided by the university, it will come in considerably cheaper – especially if the students are able to stay in university houses or halls throughout their study. Cambridge, for example, is extremely good at providing for students and most are happy to stay there for the three years.

53) PART-TIME WORK

According to the Royal Bank of Scotland's Student Cost of Living Index, London actually comes in as the most cost-effective place to study. This is because the higher wages students can earn from part-time work set off the higher cost of living. More than ten hours of work a week, however, could really affect the standard of education your child comes out with.

THE PRICE OF BOOZE

Students collectively spend nearly £1bn a year on alcohol, so it may be worth taking the cost of it into consideration. The *Push Guide to Choosing a University*, for example, has gone round the country noting the price of all student drinks. Leeds, Liverpool and Manchester all operate student bars with beer at just £1 a pint, compared to £2.10 at Westminster.

COULD IT BE CHEAPER TO STUDY OVERSEAS?

Possibly, but not tremendously. Australia, for example, is becoming more and more popular as a destination for UK students looking for an alternative to a British university. It could be worth exploring more closely but my initial investigations suggest that it won't work out so much cheaper as to warrant making a decision purely on cost. But then there could of course be other advantages or factors that could make it worth considering.

16

TRAVEL

"But automobiles are more than just a necessity to us. Our involvement with them is more than just a matter of practicality; they serve us as a symbol of freedom, strength, speed and adventure . . . In return for the freedom, independence, spontaneity, and excitement that cars are felt to give us, we have been willing to pay an enormous price – although we tend to deny the price we pay."

'The Poverty of Affluence', Paul Wachtel

Here's an interesting question for you:

From 1971 to 2003, how many more miles on average do you think people travelled within Britain? 40% more? 50% more? 60% more?

In fact, the total distance travelled by the average person in Britain has increased by an amazing 90%. Indeed, of all the different categories of spending, transport is now the highest after accommodation. People spend an average of £61 a week on getting from A to B, from C to D, and to X, Y and the big, big W.

The average household spends £3,120 on car travel alone.

So what can you do to cut down on this expense?

Well, that depends of course on how radical you want to be, how open you are to change, and how much you need or want to save.

In no particular order, here are a mix of strategies and techniques you can try.

(256) USE LESS PETROL

Cold starts can take up a lot of petrol. Instead of starting up and waiting, drive off as soon as possible. Once you're up and running, bear in mind that driving like a rally driver (mad acceleration followed by harsh braking) will burn up a lot of fuel. Drive at 60 miles an hour instead of 80 on the motorway and your petrol will last longer. If your tyres aren't at the correct pressure level you could also be burning unnecessary money.

(257) MAKE FEWER JOURNEYS

Every time you walk instead of drive you are saving money. Always plan your journey ahead to take the quickest route. Minimise journeys by combining a trip to the supermarket with a trip to B&Q or the tip instead of doing the two jobs separately.

8) SAVE A FORTUNE BY SHARING THE CAR JOURNEY TO WORK OR SCHOOL

Car sharing is now becoming a fantastically popular way to save money, reduce traffic and save the planet. One fact I read claimed that if every person were to catch a lift with someone else just once week, commuting car journeys would be reduced by 25%!

One way to organise a car share is by setting it up yourself. Ask around at work – or among the mums – to see if anyone would like to halve their petrol consumption by taking it in turns with you to do the drive there and back. Alternatively, if you do a commute, say from a village to the nearby town, ask around in the village for likely car-share candidates.

You could try some of the national and regional car share schemes that have been set up – either by internet or telephone. You simply enter the details of your journey and are then linked up with appropriate sharers. Do an internet search for car share websites for your area. On a national level, try www. liftshare.org, Tel: 08700 780225, or www.nationalcarshare. co.uk, Tel: 01344 861600.

9) GET A BIKE

When I was 20 years old I suddenly realised that two years of student life had made me about two stone overweight and horribly unhealthy. Horrified by the weight gain, I stopped eating chips twice a day and brought my old bike up from home. Several months later the weight had gone and I had developed an addiction to cycling that lasted through many years of working life in London. When I grow old I hope I will be like the 90-year-old cyclist who we used to see cycling around the Isle of Wight – amazingly fit and beaming with happiness.

I was reluctant to add this tip in because I think it takes more than a few words in a book to get a grown adult onto a bike and peddling down the road, but I promise anyone who tries it that it could completely change their life.

Before going out to buy a bike, ask around to see if anyone you know has one sitting unused in a shed or hallway. If you do buy, don't pay more than £150 – any more is just pure luxury.

260. OWN FEWER CARS

Get rid of your car altogether, or at least one of the cars you have in the household. I remember my father offering this piece of advice to a friend of his who was trying to live on a pittance and had asked him what she could do to spend less. The suggestion of getting rid of her car was at first greeted with horror and derision. However, once he made her sit down and list what she needed it for (trips to the supermarket, occasionally picking up the kids from a friend's house and visiting friends or relatives probably no more than once a month), work out how much it was costing her in total (about £2,000 a year) and then work out how much it would cost to take taxis, trains and to hire cars instead . . . the £1,000–1,500 saving a year actually did win her over.

61) DO YOU REALLY NEED A CAR AT ALL?

The truth is that for many households the cost of running a car can be crippling – yet a surprising number of people never work this out, or are unable to even imagine how doing without a car can actually be an option. It is only when you add together the cost of buying the car, fixing the car, insuring and servicing it and paying for the fuel and road tax that you realise what a large percentage of your income it can eat up.

62) EARN UP TO £200 A MONTH FROM YOUR CAR DOING NOTHING

Still not prepared to give up that second car? Still insist that you really, really need it? Then you'd better make it pay for its existence. You can get paid £66–200 a month, for example, to have a big fat advert plastered down the side of it. It will not do any damage to the paintwork. Try www.ad-wraps.co.uk or www.comm-motion.com.

63) TRY TO AVOID BUYING A CAR WITH A LOAN

Buying a car on credit can be one of the most expensive mistakes you'll ever make. Avoid it at all costs if you can and tread very carefully if you do need to borrow. It is easy to see why paying £60 a month for a car may seem like a great option, but you could very easily pay at least twice the cost of the car over the lifetime of the loan.

CHEAP WAYS TO BUY A CAR WITH A LOAN

If you *do* have to buy a car on credit, spend some time working out the cheapest way to fund the loan. Using a finance option offered by a car dealer, for example, is probably going to be the worst possible option as they now make a significant proportion of their income from flogging finance packages. The 0% finance offer may sound fantastic but is often somewhat devious to say the least. You'll probably find, in fact, that the price of the car is actually higher than if you bought it elsewhere without the finance offer.

Your best option is to look for a loan with the lowest possible APR and the shortest length that you can afford. Another option is to get a free loan by paying for the car on a credit card, then taking up all the 0% transfer offers you can get your hands on so that you never have to pay a penny in interest.

 DON'T BUY NEW CARS

What many people don't realise is that the most expensive aspect of car ownership can be in the depreciation and that this is especially true if you buy your car new. In fact, many cars will lose over half their original value in the first three years!

 BUY CARS THAT HOLD THEIR VALUE WELL

Next time you're buying a new or second-hand car, get clued up first about how well different cars hold their value. *Which?* magazine and website (www.which.co.uk) is a brilliant source of information on this subject, giving full lists of information about how much different makes and models depreciate. For example, they say:

"For an example of how crippling depreciation can be, compare the Audi A6 2.4 Quattro with the Vauxhall Omega 2.6i V6 Elite. Both are luxury cars – the Vauxhall has an on-the-road price of around £25,000 and the Audi costs about £1,000 less. But, three years down the line, you could probably recoup around £9,100 for the Audi if you sold it privately, whereas the Vauxhall would probably fetch only about £4,800. The Vauxhall will have lost roughly 80 per cent of its value."

Also:

"A new Alfa Romeo 166 will be worth just 23 per cent of its new price in three years' time. Other cars hold as much as 53 per cent of their value."

57 DO YOUR HOMEWORK BEFORE YOU BUY

In fact, without wanting to sound like a saleswoman for *Which?* magazine, I would certainly recommend that anyone check it out before buying their next car – especially as you can get a one-month trial for free! Not only will it give you extensive facts on depreciation, fuel consumption and whether or not it will cost you a fortune in repair bills, it also does a yearly list of the very best buys and the most-liked cars according to users.

In the 2005–06 report, for example:

○ Mercedes-Benz's had been discovered to be one of the worst cars for reliability in recent years, having previously been one of the very best.
○ The Toyota Yaris Verso was the most-liked small car of the year.
○ 'Don't Buys' in the medium cars category included the Fiat Stilo, the Mazda 323 and the Renault Megane.

(268) DON'T BUY A PETROL GUZZLER

The fuel consumption of similar size cars can vary as much as 45%. A Citroen C3, for example, has low fuel consumption while a Citroen Saxo is high. And, of course, choosing a smaller car over a larger one can make a massive difference to the amount of petrol you get through in a year, and your road tax.

(269) CHECK PRICE GUIDES

If you're buying a used car make sure you're not paying over the odds by checking in a price guide like the *Glass's Guide*.

The Office of Fair Trading (www.oft.gov.uk) provides a checklist for things to look out for when assessing a used car's condition. And don't assume that you'll get a better deal by going to a private seller, as this is often not the case.

Which? recommends that for a medium car for less than £5,000

"an early Ford Focus is a good buy. It comes in a range of body styles – 3- or 5-door hatchback, 4-door saloon or 5-door estate.

Engines range from 1.4- to 2.0-litre petrol and 1.8-litre diesel. Reliability is generally good and, for pre-2000 petrol models, it's excellent."

70) HOW MUCH OF IT IS ABOUT IMAGE?

During a recent holiday visiting my sister and her husband who live in Mexico City, we met some friends of theirs at a street corner. We were about to cross the road when an extremely scruffy, old red Beetle beeped its horn at us. The two people inside were an older couple who, even from a few minutes' encounter, I felt were some of the kindest, happiest, coolest and most elegant people I had ever met. As the car drove off, my sister informed us that they were an extremely wealthy couple who had driven this car for as long as anyone could remember. They were famous for giving very generously to the arts and owned some fine pieces of art themselves.

- Do we sometimes buy cars as a status symbol or as an extension of or embellishment for our personalities or lifestyle?
- Do some people spend too much money doing so?
- And do some people still buy expensive cars in an attempt to keep up with the Jones's?

Most probably we do.

All I am saying here is that if you want your car to say something positive about you, it's a lot cheaper to aim for the bohemian image described above than it is to spend a fortune on a brand-new dream machine.

(271) DON'T BUY ANYTHING TOO POSH OR FLASH

As a general rule, the smarter the car you buy the more it will cost you in both grief and money. In the story above, for example, we were walking to the supermarket because the brand-new car my sister had bought had been stolen just five days after they'd bought it. The smarter the car, the higher the insurance. The more electrical gadgets it has, the more costly trips you'll make to the garage. And just imagine how upset you'd be when the hooligan up the road decides to run a metal bar along the side of it.

(272) USE AIR CONDITIONING SPARINGLY

It increases fuel consumption significantly.

(273) SPEND LESS ON INSURANCE

Always shop around. Never make a claim on your insurance unless you're sure that the cost of the repair is more than the excess you'll have to pay or the value of the no-claims discount you'll lose. You may be able to get a discount from some insurers if you take the advanced driving test (see www.iam.org.uk, Tel: 020 8996 9600). Always tell your insurer if you drive fewer than 12,000 miles a year or don't use your car to commute to work.

CUTTING THE COST OF TRAIN JOURNEYS

(274) TRAIN TICKETS FOR HALF THE PRICE

If you're making a journey by train, try to book your tickets as far ahead as six weeks before you want to make the journey, and as soon as possible if you don't make it as early as that. Most train companies will release a small number of cheaper tickets for most journeys but you will often need to book early to get them. APEX tickets, for example, are normally the cheapest tickets available. Ring the train company to enquire about the cheapest tickets they issue and how you can get them. Bear in mind, though, that if you book some of these cheap tickets, they are non-transferable, so you can only travel on the train you have booked.

275) GET SEASON TICKETS

If you travel by train regularly, you can buy weekly, monthly, or even yearly season tickets in advance. And if you have to park at the train station, you will often find that you can buy season tickets for parking too.

276) TRAIN TICKETS AT A THIRD OFF

If you have any children, make sure you buy a Family Railcard. It costs £20 and entitles adults to 1/3 off, children to 60% off. Simply ask for a form at your local train station.

277) CHEAT YOUR WAY TO CHEAPER TRAIN TICKETS

On some routes you can actually save money by buying two tickets instead of one. On a journey from Birmingham to Bristol, for example, a standard return costs £56. If you buy a return from Birmingham to Cheltenham and then another one from Cheltenham to Bristol, you can save £26.

TRAVEL BY COACH TO SAVE HUNDREDS OF POUNDS A YEAR

There is no denying that travelling by coach is often a far cheaper option. A standard rail return between London and Exeter, for example, would probably set you back about £55. A similar journey by National Express coaches on the other hand would cost you just £32.50, or as little as £11.00 if you buy a 'funfare' from the www.nationalexpress.com website.

 GET COACH TICKETS FOR AS LITTLE AS 50P

If you're travelling to or from London, buying coach tickets from Megabus (www.megabus.com) is almost always going to be your cheapest option. In fact, if you're travelling off-peak, you can even get your ticket for as little as the booking fee of 50p! At the time of writing, for example, you could get a fare from London to Bristol for £5.50, Southampton to London for £7.00, Aberdeen to London for just £17.

17

LEISURE AND PLEASURE

○ Do something better with your life
○ Have more sex, mend a hedge or become a novelist
○ Get free accommodation, cheaper holidays and save the planet

In talking to people while researching this book, I have found that one of the main reasons people give for their over-spending is that they need to spend money in order to enjoy themselves and have a great life.

The truth is that we would all like more money so that we can enjoy a better life and I would certainly not deny that having money to spend on leisure can bring a lot of pleasure.

If happiness, contentment and the ability to enjoy a full and meaningful life are our main aims, however, then there are plenty of ways of getting those for free or for a lot less money.

MAKE THE MOST OF FREE ACTIVITIES

 280 GO LOCAL

Make a list of all the places that are free to visit in your area. Pin the list to the kitchen wall and you'll have something fun to do next time you find yourself bored of a weekend. This could include museums, galleries and other local attractions, but also consider things like taking a walk along a nearby beach, canal or deserted railway track, picnics in the countryside, picking blackberries, watching the local buskers or learning about the architecture in your town.

281 CREATE NEW ADVENTURES

To make exciting things happen in your life, get out and about to as many new places as possible. In his book 'The Luck Factor', Richard Wiseman, from the psychology department at the University of Hertfordshire, tells us that it is often chance meetings or chance occurrences that can have a significant, life-changing effect on our future. One single, unplanned event can have a massive effect on our career, relationship or even health or happiness. During a visit to a local museum, for example, you may come across an idea that inspires you to a total career change. A visit to a museum or golf course could be the place where you meet a future spouse. A chance chat with the CEO in the lift could open up a new career level for you.

Go to old places and new places. Talk to people you know and people you don't. And always go with a receptive state of mind.

82 TAKE UP A NEW HOBBY OR JUST DO SOMETHING CREATIVE

Take an evening course in furniture making or write a script for a new TV show. Borrow the kids' paint set and spend an hour 'expressing yourself' one night. Or better still, you know all those things you think of doing when you have more leisure time one day. Well what about doing them now? And who knows, your new hobby may turn into an exciting new career. The photographer Julia Margaret Cameron took up photography at the age of 50. The novelist Mary Wesley didn't start writing novels until she was in her 70s.

83 HAVE MORE SEX

The actress Mae West claimed that "an orgasm a day keeps the doctor away". The Tantric Buddhists believe that it is impossible to achieve enlightenment without practising Tantric yoga. And now scientists seem to have shown that having sex with a loving partner is one of the most important factors affecting our level of happiness.

An extensive study carried out by Dartmouth College economist David Blanchflower and Andrew Oswald of the University of Warwick showed that sex is so important for our satisfaction with life that increasing intercourse from once a month to once a week is equivalent to the amount of happiness generated by getting an extra £20,000 or £30,000 income!

The most important thing is that if you do feel like you're not getting enough, you have to find a way to solve the problem – even if it means getting yourself to a bookshop, library or

Amazon to pick up some tips. Many therapists recommend scheduling an exact time and date for having a night of passion. Californian psychologist Bernie Zilbergeld says that it's all about bringing fun back into your relationship. Make time to have a night out together and do the things you did when you were dating that were really fun.

(284) AVOID EXPENSIVE GYM MEMBERSHIP FEES

Cycle to work instead of going to the gym to save hundreds of pounds a year. Buy a fitness video and do it at home. Organise a group of friends as an after-dark or even lunchtime jogging club. Join a fitness class once or twice a week – it's a lot more fun than the running machine. Or simply walk up the stairs instead of using the escalator.

(285) ENJOY A FEW HOURS AT THE LOCAL LIBRARY

Browsing in a library can have more charm than browsing in a bookshop and you never waste money buying books that you never really read, or that didn't have much more to say than the summary on the jacket. You can also hire free (or nearly free) DVDs or videos.

(286) CONSIDER VOLUNTARY WORK

Want a sense of meaning in your life? Then consider some voluntary work. If I told you to take on some extra work for which you will not get paid, you might tell me to stuff it up my jumper. Yet every year, hundreds of thousands of people discover just how wonderful it can be to do some form of voluntary work. Whether it's spending just an hour a week talking to an elderly person down the road, becoming a school governor or teaching a once-a-week class, or even travelling to the third world to 'do some good', becoming a volunteer can be amazingly satisfying and invigorating. It can be great to spend some time doing something that's totally outside your normal life. It could be a chance to get involved with something that you really love. Doing something for the benefit of others can also give you a real sense of meaning.

○ Volunteering England is a great organisation to contact to start finding out just what kind of opportunities could be open to you. You can ring them on 0845 305 6979 or try their website at www.volunteering.org.uk.

○ Green Volunteers (www.greenvolunteers.com) is a directory of wildlife conservation projects and organisations throughout the world (looking after black bears in Minnesota or studying great white sharks in South Africa, for example).

○ Voluntary Services Overseas (www.vso.org.uk) is a charity which sends people to developing countries throughout the world to share their skills.

(287) GO THE CINEMA

I know this isn't free, but it strikes me as far better to spend £7 on the cinema than £15.99 on a DVD. Most cinemas do bargain nights on a Monday or Tuesday.

GET FREE TRIPS TO SEE PLAYS AND CONCERTS AND EVEN HOLIDAYS

Organise trips to see events in big cities and you can go along for free. All you need to do is advertise to find a group of people then book the tickets, transport and perhaps even a hotel. As the organiser of the event you will be able to go along for free. Once you've got this under your belt, you could even expand to arranging group holidays.

 LOOK OUT FOR DISCOUNTED TICKETS AND DEALS

These days you rarely need to pay full price for theatre, theme parks and other leisure activities. There are many sites online which offer packages such as theatre and hotel, dinner and comedy night deals, for example. You can also get cheap standby theatre tickets if you try to buy them on the day, and '2 for 1' offers on other activities like spa days.

 GET FREE TICKETS TO TV SHOWS

There are a lot of TV shows these days where a large audience is integral to the show. What you may be surprised to learn is that you can get tickets to most of these shows for free simply by contacting the agency that's dealing with it. See the BBC website at www.bbc.co.uk/whatson/tickets, or try Powerhouse Film and TV at www.werhousetv.co.uk.

FIND ALTERNATIVES TO EATING OUT

Judging by the number of restaurants everywhere, eating out has become one of the nation's favourite pastimes. Need something to do or somewhere to meet up with friends? It's easy to default to the habit of meeting up for a meal. Your suggestions of alternative activities, however, will no doubt be gladly met by both your family and friends. How about just doing something like wall climbing, the cinema or a night in playing Trivial Pursuit together instead? Alternatives for night-time dining might include a fondue party or a creative cooking night at home.

292 EAT OUT CHEAPER

During the day, instead of arranging to meet up with friends in a pub or restaurant, join them in a beautiful or exciting place for a picnic instead. If you've got kids with you, make sure you come equipped with games they can play or even set up a treasure hunt. Then there's fish and chips on the beach, hot dogs at the ice-skating rink or hamburgers at a local car boot sale, or soup from thermos flasks followed by a walk across the hills together.

If you can't avoid the restaurant, set a budget for yourself and choose something that rounds up to that price. For example, a starter for £3.80, a main meal for £8.75, and a dessert for £4.95 falls nicely under £20. Don't neglect the cost of your drinks too.

HOLIDAYS

293 SET YOURSELF A BUDGET

According to a recent survey, *the average cost of a family holiday abroad is now £2,725*. If you don't set yourself a budget for your holiday it is very easy for expenses to escalate and for it to end up costing you a fortune. Pick your location carefully by weighing up the cost of travel, accommodation and expenses like food and drink once you get there.

294 BE AWARE OF THE DAMAGE DONE TO THE ENVIRONMENT BY EVERY FLIGHT YOU MAKE

The average return flight, per person, creates roughly the same amount of CO_2 as the average car creates in a year. If we don't reduce our carbon emissions drastically over the coming decade the effect on the world we live in could be catastrophic. Do your bit, reduce the number of flights you make.

295 NEVER PAY FOR HOTELS AGAIN

HomeLink International (www.homelink.org.uk) is a fantastic company that enables you to enjoy free accommodation (and even the use of a car) all over the world by swapping your home with another family for a few weeks. Flying to Italy, for example, can be very cheap these days yet the accommodation when you get there can be very pricey. Visit HomeLink's website, however, and search for home swap options all over the country. The site gives you preferred dates, destinations the other home would like to swap for, how many people it sleeps and whether or not a car exchange is also available. Countries include Australia, Canada, Mexico and the US and there are 13,500 members around the world.

6) EXHILARATING HOLIDAYS FOR £65 A WEEK

The National Trust (www.nationaltrust.org.uk) offer an amazing opportunity to get a holiday in beautiful surroundings for approximately £60 a week including food and hostel-type accommodation. In return for your board you will have to put in a lot of labour that may include coppicing woods, herding goats or painting a lighthouse. But for a certain type of person this may actually be a benefit in itself. Certainly beats taking a week off to sit at home wasting your life away on eBay.

7) SAVE MONEY AND THE PLANET

When travelling to poorer, developing countries, make sure your money goes to locals rather than multinational companies. Stay in locally owned accommodation, use public transport and buy local goods rather than imported.

8) VISIT FRIENDS AND FAMILY

Almost everybody has a friend they could go and stay with as a holiday. The money you'll save on accommodation could make it a lot cheaper – especially as you also won't have the need to eat out for every meal. Your friends and family will probably appreciate the visit as well.

9) THE HOLIDAY OF A LIFETIME FOR THE PRICE OF A SHORT BREAK IN PARIS

Taking one big holiday in a faraway country can actually be a cheaper way of holidaying than having a few shorter trips within England and Europe, for two reasons. First of all, if you're travelling in developing countries like Cambodia or Ecuador, everything you have to pay for once you get there will be so much cheaper that it will make up for the more expensive price of the flight. Secondly, a short trip to Paris in April will leave you hungering for another holiday by June at the very latest. Two weeks in Cuba could give you enough buzz and colourful memories to keep you going for the next 18 months.

Lonely Planet publishes a whole series of Shoestring Guides to help you plan an amazing adventure on a tight budget. It's not just for students!

(300) FIND THE CHEAPEST FLIGHT WITH JUST ONE SEARCH

If you're looking for the cheapest flight or hotel, visit www. travelsupermarket.com. You can search all the big sites including Opodo, Lastminute, Ryanair and Easyjet at the same time.

(301) AN EVEN SMARTER WAY TO GET CHEAP FLIGHTS

Sometimes it can be cheaper – and/or with more convenient times – to buy two different singles from two different airlines. Fly out with Easyjet, and back with Ryanair, for example.

(302) BOOK YOUR HOLIDAYS FURTHER IN ADVANCE

Instead of waiting till July to book your holiday in August, you can save yourself a lot of money if you start looking around and shopping for deals in, say, March. Cheap flight companies, for example, release a small number of tickets at cheaper prices on a first come, first served basis. Also with hotels or European cottages, you'll get more for your money if you don't leave it too late to book the best and therefore most popular ones.

PAY FOR YOUR HOLIDAY BY IMPORTING GOODS

If you go on holiday to places like Turkey, India or Malaysia, for example, you could actually pay for the cost of your holiday by doing a bit of importing trade while you're out there. You may want to look around the shops in your town and even talk to the owners to find out the kind of things that would be appropriate. If you do consider this option, you will need to take it seriously and plan properly.

GO TO THE BEST RESTAURANTS IN TOWN FOR JUST £10

When you're on holiday, eating out is one of the nicest pleasures and it is a joy to eat at the very best places. One way of enjoying the top locations and restaurants is to take just a drink there or a dessert and coffee. Even at the most expensive establishments this shouldn't cost more than £10 or £15 but you'll get to enjoy the same atmosphere and feeling of luxury as those who may be paying £100 a head for their meal.

ENJOY THE BEST HOTELS AROUND THE WORLD FOR JUST £20 A DAY

Along the same principles, wherever you are on holiday in the world, seek out the most gorgeous and sumptuous hotels and have an afternoon drink in the bar there. After a day of sight-seeing, the calm oasis of a beautiful, air-conditioned hotel will transform your holiday, your nerves and your feeling of being pampered. And don't worry – they will let you in!

(306) CENTRAL LONDON ACCOMMODATION FROM £19.50 PER PERSON PER NIGHT!

It's a little-known fact that university halls of residence rent out rooms and self-contained flats to holidaymakers from the beginning of June to the middle of September. The University of Westminster, for example, offers rooms in the West End, Victoria, Waterloo and the City. Contact them on 0207 911 5000.

(307) DISCOUNT HOTEL WEBSITES

If you do fancy a swankier option for a weekend in the City, never book directly with the hotel. Visit a website such as www.hotelslondon.co.uk instead where you can get expensive hotels at a 50% discount or more.

(308) JOIN THE NATIONWIDE BANK TO GET CHEAPEST RATES WHEN WITHDRAWING MONEY OVERSEAS

A survey by *The Guardian* recently revealed huge differences between the charges levied by different banks to customers withdrawing money from ATMs overseas. HSBC was charging 4.4%, for example, Lloyds TSB 4% and NatWest and Royal Bank of Scotland 5.5%. The Nationwide in contrast charged its customers no fees at all.

18

HAPPINESS THAT MONEY CAN'T BUY

In the Theatre of the Absurd play 'Rhinoceros' by French author Eugene Ionesco, everybody in the community slowly starts turning into rhinoceros. At first it is just a few running madly through the streets, and a group of people in the play stand outside a grocer's shop discussing the madness that is going on. But then, person by person, everybody else succumbs, almost as if they don't even notice the change. At the end of the play only the lead character, Berenger, is left and he vows not to be lured into becoming a blundering, hungry, aggressive rhinoceros as well.

Written in 1958, 'Rhinoceros' was Ionesco's response to the rise of fascism and the difficulty of maintaining one's individuality in the face of an overwhelming force of social change. While I would probably be lynched if I actually tried to equate fascism with the blind and frenzied hunger for material wealth in today's society, I believe there are some similarities.

Like the good people who become rhinos in the play, it is not because we are bad that we are constantly filled with desire to buy, buy, buy. It is not because we are bad at heart that we believe that being able to afford more and more expensive things is our best route towards increased happiness.

This is the happiness that has been sold to us by the capitalist culture we live in. And once again it is not because capitalism itself is bad. It is because by making its first and foremost goal material advancement and enhancement, it has lost sight of other important things along the way.

In fact, if most of us sat down and thought it through, we would be the first to admit that money can't buy us happiness. We have just somehow along the way been fooled into believing that it can.

The happiness you get from buying a shiny big new car or cute little iPod is wonderful at first. It appears on your face like a bright light and a huge, excited smile. But then it begins to fade and a few months later you're carrying it around as a grey heaviness that sits in your cheek, an extra weight that is dragging down your life.

The presence of true happiness, however, is a light that is always shining inside you – a feeling that the way you're living your life is absolutely right.

"In my work, I meet more and more business people who secretly despise the system they are a part of, who deplore the lack of corporate values, who know their products and services are of little consequence, and who would love to be out of it and do something more meaningful; but they have a mortgage and a Mercedes to service, and two point four children in private education who would feel deprived and vulnerable without the latest in brand-name clothing that their peers

*all parade in. It takes courage to step out of the line — more
than most can muster. So they don their suit and tie and serve
the system, but they glance more often out of the window.
The spirit is stirring in such people, and they are
increasingly asking themselves tough questions."*

Sir John Whitmore

So what is the solution?

Take back the really truly valuable things in life that are yours
by right. Making a stand against the more negative side of mass
consumption and materialism doesn't need to mean giving up
your job or the creature comforts or even the more beautiful of
the luxuries you enjoy. It can start with just a seizing of more
of the non-material joys of life.

09 STANDING STILL TO ENJOY THE NIGHT SKY OR THE BLOWING OF THE WIND

*"To persons standing alone on a hill during a clear midnight
such as this, the roll of the world eastward is almost a
palpable movement."*

'Far from the Madding Crowd', Thomas Hardy

10 HAVING A PEACEFUL MIND

Take time out one evening a week to attend a class in yoga, meditation or tai chi – the change in mind you can get from these
activities can be like taking a mind-altering drug. Seek help
(from self-help books or professionals) if you feel emotionally

disturbed or troubled in your life. Talk to your GP if you think you may actually be depressed or dangerously over-stressed. Read a book about buddhism. Do what you need to do to solve that feeling inside you that says something's not quite right.

 FEELING PROUD OF THE PERSON THAT YOU ARE

Whoever that may be.

 GOOD HEALTH

How much money would you exchange for the promise of good health for the rest of a long life? In her book 'Life Coaching: Change Your Life in Seven Days', Eileen Mulligan says that each of us makes the mistake of concentrating too much on certain areas of our life and ignoring or not paying enough attention to the rest. The areas she lists are: Health, The Spiritual, Work and Career, Finances, Personal Relationships, Family and Social Life. To live in a happy and healthy state you need to work at a balance of all of these areas. Our health, however, is one we so often overlook.

Why?

Because looking after your health is seen as just a boring old preventative measure that may or may not pay you dividends in the future. As every fit and health-conscious person knows, however, looking after your health pays you massive dividends today. If you eat really healthily, exercise regularly and enjoy a good work–life balance, you will have more energy and vigour for life. The components of a healthy life themselves – preparing fresh vegetables, long walks, active relaxation and fresh air – will massively improve your enjoyment of life in themselves. For many people suffering from depression, regular exercise could even be the best form of therapy.

ELEGANCE

You don't need to have lots of money to look and feel fantastic. Stand up straight and wear your clothes and your life with elegance and pride.

LEARN HOW TO RECOGNISE SOME OF THE DIFFERENT STARS AND CONSTELLATIONS IN THE SKY

The Milky Way alone contains some 200 billion suns and belongs to a cluster of 30 other galaxies within 2.5 million light years from each other. There are thousands of such clusters scattered throughout space. Take a chair and sit out in your garden one night. Watch the sky and realise how big and truly peaceful, yet alive, it can make you feel. Better still, arm yourself with a book that helps you spot the constellations and make this a regular habit.

BEING NICE TO OTHER PEOPLE

Go out of your way to say something to somebody that you know will give them an extra glow of happiness all weekend. Ring somebody up out of the blue and tell them that you miss them. Write somebody a letter. Decide to pursue a line of work where you will be doing something to improve the lot of society or humanity.

HAVING TIME TO DO THE REALLY LIFE- ENHANCING AND MEANINGFUL THINGS IN LIFE

"Dust if you must, but wouldn't it be better to paint a picture, or write a letter, bake a cake, or plant a seed. Ponder the difference between want and need.

Dust if you must, but there's not much time, with rivers to swim and mountains to climb! Music to hear, and books to read, friends to cherish and life to lead.

Dust if you must, but the world's out there with the sun in your eyes, the wind in your hair, a flutter of snow, a shower of rain, this day will not come round again.

Dust if you must, but bear in mind, old age will come and its not kind. And when you go, and go you must, you, yourself, will make more dust!"

Anonymous

 SILENCE

Stop for a minute and enjoy the silence. Listen hard to what it says. Look out of a window and seek out corners where it lies. Close your eyes and imagine the silence of the galaxies out in space. Spend five minutes doing nothing but watching a child playing, your spouse cooking or your own hand writing. Try it tonight.

7) SPEND TIME WITH NATURE

It is totally free and perhaps the most soothing and invigorating thing you can do for your mind and your soul. Pop out more often for a five-minute think in the garden. Borrow a book about trees and take a walk with it in the woods. Grow something from seed in a pot on your desk. Take a tent and camp out in a field somewhere.

8) WORK ON YOUR RELATIONSHIPS

Work on your relationship with your partner or spouse – or just really appreciate how much you enjoy having them around. Don't only tell them that you love them more often, also tell them the reasons why. And do things to show them just how much you appreciate their existence or the hard work they do for you.

Don't spend enough good time together? Then that will have to change. Don't get enough time apart? Then it's time to change that too. Problems that need solving? Then seek solutions or help. The problems will not just go away unless you do something to solve them.

Spend more time with friends and nurture new friendships. After a good relationship with a spouse, it's probably the second most important ingredient for a happy contented life.

9) AND, MOST IMPORTANTLY OF ALL, CONCENTRATE ON A DIFFERENT KIND OF GROWTH

As human beings we have an intrinsic desire to be upwardly mobile. We always want to be moving forward, improving ourselves and bettering our place in life. In a society that concentrates on financial, material and technological advancement, the easiest translation or focus for that urge is in earning more money, having more things, living in a bigger house or having a better car, computer or telly.

But could things be different?

What if we were to concentrate on spiritual or inner growth instead? What if we were to aim to be better, happier, kinder and more deeply fulfilled people? What if we were to concentrate on growing towards where we want to be as people in our inner life – rather than where we want to be in terms of the price of our property, the money in the bank or the size of our salary?

And I'm not saying that the two need to be mutually exclusive – only that we should always check that the first is not getting in the way of the latter.

19

CREATING MORE TIME IN YOUR LIFE

○ The top four things that can steal or waste our time
○ Make sure you're getting at least one really, really good hour out of every single day
○ Understanding what it is that you really want to have more time for

I imagine that, a hundred years ago, the term 'killing time' was used far more frequently than it is today. After all, how many working people these days have time to kill? Indeed, if you are reading this chapter it is presumably because for you the reverse is actually true.

Oh, what I wouldn't give to have some time to kill. And I would kill it so softly it would cover me in goose bumps.

"Play it, Sam. Play 'As Time Goes By'."

said Humphrey Bogart in Casablanca (not "Play it again, Sam" as is commonly thought). And time, it has to be said, certainly does go by.

But surely it is not how much we manage to fit into our lives that really matters but what we do with the hours we have and how much we enjoy them. When people say that they wish they had more time, I think what their whole being is actually calling out for is for them to lead their lives either just very slightly or quite dramatically differently. Perhaps it might be just a slight alteration in attitude or expectations that is being called for – or a complete rethink about where their life is heading.

The four biggest destroyers, wasters and thieves of our precious lives surely have to be:

TIME WASTER NO. 1: NAGGING DISSATISFACTION

If you feel that something is somehow wrong – be it in your life, your relationship, your job or other – it will eat up your time like no other. You will fill the day with activities that get you nowhere. You will spend hours vaguely fretting without really having any focus to your fretting. You could spend the whole day just watching your life go by wishing that somehow it was just an awful lot different. However hard you work, whatever you do, you don't seem to be getting anywhere.

Solution?

You have to make a very bold move and bring about a very big change in your life.

TIME WASTER NO. 2: SAVING TIME

I know it may sound crazy to say that time-saving measures steal our time away from us but consider this: What exactly is it that we are saving the time for? If I drive to the shops instead of taking a walk then I am missing the opportunity to watch other people pass by and feel the world slowly turn on its axis as I saunter down the street. If I have a readymade pasta sauce for dinner I am wasting the opportunity to chop fresh tomatoes and parsley and smell the different fresh ingredients as they slowly melt together in the pot. If I email my friend instead of writing them a letter, I am missing the opportunity to enjoy one of the most cathartic and beautiful activities known to man.

When I decided to give up buying meat from the supermarket and get it from the butchers instead, the 20 minutes I now spend in the butchers every Friday has become one of the highlights of my week. Today, for example, I bought a local pheasant for £2.99 and had a great chat with another customer about how best to cook it. Did you know that before Christmas you're better off just wrapping them in streaky bacon and shoving them in the oven for an hour? When they start getting tougher in January, soften up the meat by cooking them in a casserole with some red wine or Madeira.

TIME WASTER NO. 3: WORKING

Everybody has to work for a living and there's no getting away from it. In fact, the satisfaction of working hard to put bread on the table is a core ingredient of all human happiness. But doing your job should not get in the way of living. Doing your job should be one of the good things about living. And your work should not be so consuming that it prevents you from keeping your whole life in balance.

323 TIME WASTER NO. 4: TELEVISION

Ever thought that you could have more time to do better things if you didn't spend most evenings sat in front of the television? Then try an experiment: Turn off the telly and face the silence. You'll be amazed by what you can manage to fill that time up with. There are two big whole wonderful empty hours between 9 and 11.

Turn on the telly to watch a certain programme and before you know it it's 12 o'clock, you're late for bed again and you've watched two hours of rubbish. I know it can be really hard to press that button but it might just be worth doing.

LIVE LIFE AS IF YOU ONLY HAD A FEW MONTHS LEFT OF IT

"As if you could kill time without injuring eternity,"

said Henry David Thoreau. Remember that you only have one life, and it's a cliché I know, but you really ought to live life as if you only had a few months left of it. Make time to do things that will add real value to your life – things that will make you feel like the person you want to be, the person you would like to be remembered as when you die.

324 MAKE ARRANGEMENTS TO DO THINGS

A swim in the local pool? An evening class in pottery or Renaissance literature? Or a martini cocktail with a rarely seen friend? We can spend months (years) wishing, we had time to do these things yet actually be doing very little with our evenings instead. If you simply take the plunge and schedule these things in, you'll be amazed by how much you really can fit into your life. Don't wait for the motivation to come that will make you pick up the phone and make the arrangement because you'll be waiting all year. You have to force yourself to start with the action. The motivation will only come when you're sat behind that bar or potter's wheel.

Still don't think you've got the energy? If they are pleasurable and relaxing activities, then they will actually make you feel less tired.

25) HOW TO LITERALLY SLOW DOWN TIME

Scientists have observed that we spend a lot less time looking at the things that we see than we did 50 years ago. It is, therefore, not so much that the world is moving faster but that we are speeding up the way in which we experience it. To reverse this effect, all you have to do is spend longer looking at the things that you see in the day – be it a favourite picture on a wall, a cloud in the sky or the key of a piano. Learn to look at more things for a minimum of a full five seconds and you can significantly increase your enjoyment of, and passion for, life.

26) STOP READING NEWSPAPERS

If you currently spend quite a significant chunk of your day reading newspapers, take a good look at this habit. Is all that reading adding enough pleasure to your life to justify the time you spend on it – or are you spending too much time on this activity out of habit? Would your time be better spent reading books or magazines instead, or doing something completely different?

327 CREATE TIME FOR EXERCISE

Create time for exercise and it will magically feel as if you've been given an extra dimension of time in the day. Walk or cycle to work and feel the benefits of a clear head when you get there. Walk to the shops. Go to the swimming pool before dinner in the evening. Get somebody to babysit once a week and go and do some kind of exciting sport or hobby.

328 CREATE TIME FOR IMPORTANT AND BREAKTHROUGH IDEAS

Create time for important and breakthrough ideas – both at work and in your private life. Regularly spend an hour in a room with nothing but a pen and paper. Your aim is to get breakthrough ideas to flow that would never have come other-wise under normal timepressured circumstances.

329 DON'T TRY SO HARD AND YOU WILL GET MORE DONE

Dr Robert Kriegel, leading expert in the field of human per-formance and change and former coach to Olympic athletes, says that a lot of people try to work too hard. In experiments with sales teams, for example, he has told half the group to make as many calls as they can, the other half to make fewer calls than they would normally. Without fail he finds that the results from the group that made fewer calls are far better than the group that made more.

ASK FOR MORE TIME

Whether it's your boss, your spouse or the person who sits opposite you chatting all day ... you won't get more time unless you ask.

PEEL A CARROT REALLY, REALLY SLOWLY

We can waste our lives away wishing we had more time to enjoy ourselves. Remember, though, that the greatest pleasure in life comes from slowing down and enjoying what you are doing right now. Whether it's typing on your keyboard, peeling a carrot or reading a story to your child, slow down and really live inside the moment. Watch every single moment carefully as it magically unfolds.

WE'RE ALL DOING TOO MUCH

French psychologist Christophe Dejours has recognised that many of us are suffering from what he calls 'pathologies of overloading'. Overactivity, he says, is making people ill. We have too much to do. Too much pressure. And to borrow the phrase from sociologist Alain Ehrenberg, we are suffering from the 'fatigue of being oneself'.

333 MINI-BREAKS

Force yourself to take a series of mini-breaks during the day when you take a little bit of time that's just for you to enjoy. Learn to say 'No' to some things that you don't want to do. Be aware of how often you tell yourself to 'Hurry up' and instead replace the instruction with 'Relax and slow down'. You may actually find that by slowing down you can get more done.

20

YOUR 'JOB' OR YOUR 'WORK'

○ Pack in your job and become an organic gardener?
○ Ask your boss for a four-day week?
○ Or is there something else you've been wanting to tell them?

"Should I be doing something better with my life?"

This is such a monumentally important question (after all, you've only got one stab at life on this earth and if you don't get round to answering it very soon then you'll be dead in a coffin before you do) that most people actually choose to ignore it.

Although 'choose' suggests too much of an active decision being involved here. The word we're looking for, in fact, is 'procrastination'.

Just as yet another year can pass by before you get round to painting your bedroom or fixing the lock in the bathroom, so you can continue to drift through your life in the same old groove until you look in the mirror one day and realise that you're 70.

So what does a book about 'Spend Less, Live Better' advocate when it comes to working?

Well, first of all it hopes not to advocate anything. Each person is very different in what they enjoy and what they want to get from life. What this book does believe in, however, is enjoying life as much as possible. Now. Today. Not some time in the future when you've got more money.

If your work or job doesn't actively increase your enjoyment of life, then something is wrong, or missing. If long hours are making your enjoyment of life suffer then something needs changing. If you're working yourself bloodless to sustain an expensive lifestyle, then that expensive lifestyle sure as hell better be worth it. And if lack of money is destroying you, then perhaps you may need to find a better way of earning – or making what you do have go further.

Some years ago, there was an incredible piece of graffiti that appeared on a fence along the M40 from Oxford to London. In letters over a metre high and at a length of at least some 30 metres were written the words:

"WHY DO I DO THIS EVERY DAY?"

This was probably carried out by some smug person on the dole goofing off with a bottle of cider in his pocket. However, I prefer to imagine some besuited gentleman climbing over stiles with a big pot of paint in his hand, and daubing his final salute of warning to his fellow commuters before setting off to become a sheep farmer in New Zealand.

(334) WHY DO WE WORK SO MUCH?

Americans, as you know, are notorious for working hellishly long hours, being the ultimate consumerist society and for worshipping at the shrine of Mammon. However, they also have a history of people rebelling against this lifestyle and campaigning for a return to simplicity.

The Amish people, for example, shun the whole idea of cars, tellies and having a 'job'. Work for them instead is working in the fields, preparing meals or sitting down to sew by lamplight of an evening. Simple pleasures are essential to the Amish way of life, so harvesting barley in the sunshine or strapping your horse into its carriage are both the way you make your living and your enjoyment of earthly paradise.

And then, of course, there is the famous Henry D. Thoreau. A 19th century poet and philosopher born to a reasonably wealthy family, Thoreau chose a lifestyle of voluntary simplicity in order to amplify the intellectual and spiritual richness in his life. When he wrote his most famous work, 'Walden' in 1845–47, he spent two years living alone by a pond with nothing more than his thoughts and the labour of his hands. Needing only six weeks of labour a year to grow the food he needed to eat, the rest of his time was left for reflection and living:

"Sometimes, on a summer morning, having taken my accustomed bath, I sat in my sunny doorway from sunrise till noon, rapt in a reverie, amidst the pines and hickories and sumachs, in undisturbed solitude and stillness, while the birds sung around or flitted noiseless through the house, until by the sun falling in at my west window, or the noise of some traveller's wagon on the distant highway, I was reminded of the lapse of time. I grew in those seasons like corn in the night, and they were far better than any work of the hands would have been. They were not time subtracted from my life, but

so much over and above my usual allowance. I realised what
the Orientals mean by contemplation and the forsaking of
works. For the most part, I minded not how the hours went.
The day advanced as if to light some work of mine; it was
morning, and lo, now it is evening, and nothing memorable
is accomplished. Instead of singing like the birds, I silently
smiled at my incessant good fortune. As the sparrow
had its trill, sitting on the hickory before my door, so had
I my chuckle or suppressed warble which he might hear
out of my nest."

(335) LIVE YOUR DREAM

Some years ago, a good friend of mine packed in his well-paid job as a manager in sales to live his dream of becoming a ski instructor. Living at first off just the money he made from renting out his apartment after paying the mortgage, he and his (now) wife lived in ski resorts in France, Andorra and Chile. Living the life they wanted to lead meant having to watch the pennies and fix snow chains to the tyres of their Volvo just to drive to the local supermarket. It has also enabled them to travel the world, spend days on end just skiing and work only part-time jobs, and Mark is now a fully qualified ski instructor with several years of teaching under his very happy belt.

In his book, 'What should I Do with My Life?', author Po Bronson tells the stories of people who have done incredible things to change and redirect their lives. Sidney is a 70-year-old ex-professor of chemistry who started a career in law in his sixties sings regularly in choirs and often walks the two and a half miles from his home in Islington to his chambers near Chancery Lane. Katt, at the age of 32, retrained as the brilliant shot putter she had been at the age of 19 – good enough to try for the Olympics. Rick, a corporate lawyer, left his career at the age of 38 to become a long-distance truck driver – to start being alive to life again and to dedicate himself more to his adopted son.

Says Rick:

*"Your job runs your entire life. I had a permanent edginess
back then . . . I used to think six lines all the time.
And stupidly I was proud of it. I thought it was who
I was, but I see now it was a symptom of my work.
And I see now that multitasking creates a sense of guilt that
you're selling everyone short, including yourself . . .
I have autonomy (now). I have a window seat with
a view that changes every mile. Nobody ever comes into my
office without asking. I enjoy this job, but I'll be the
first to admit that it's not like what you do. It's not my
passion. I'm doing this for the wages, and I'm doing this
because it doesn't eat me alive."*

EMBRACE CHANGE

Human beings by nature do not like change. We will stick with the devil we know rather than search out the angels we don't. We will spend every day of our life moaning about something without really doing anything to change it.

BE PREPARED TO JUMP OUT ON A LIMB

As Po Bronson says:

> "*Do not wait for the kind of clarity that comes with epiphanies. In the nine hundred plus stories I heard in my research, almost nobody was struck with an epiphany . . . Don't doubt your desire because it comes to you as a whisper; don't think, 'If it were really important to me, I'd feel clearer about this, less conflicted.' My research didn't show that to be true. The things we really want to do are usually the ones that scare us the most. The things you'll not feel conflicted about are the choices that leave no one hurt.*"

 USE SPENDING LESS TO ESCAPE THE TYRANNY OF WORK

One of the obvious side-effects of learning how to spend less is that it can make you far less of a prisoner of your job – or actually help you to enjoy your current job more. The more you spend and the more debt you take in, the more dependent upon your job you become. Worse still, if you are constantly feeling that you (still) don't earn enough to be able to afford your lifestyle, then you may get an almost desperate need to earn more or get promoted, despite actually being happy where you are in your work.

By cutting back on spending and getting firmly in the black, you can feel much more comfortable about where you are and where you want to go. Needing money less could enable a high-earning over-worker to quit his or her job and take on a more life-affirming job instead. It could enable another person to quit the job he hates and take off on a working holiday around the world for a year. Or it could enable yet a third person to realise that they are actually happy in their lower-paid job – and that the rewards it offers are worth the small hardship of having to watch the pennies.

CHOOSING TO WORK LESS TO LIVE MORE

Voluntarily deciding to take a pay cut may seem pretty crazy, but more and more people these days are opting to do it. They are also discovering that they can live on less money and actually live a better life for it.

○ Is it really worth working till 8 o'clock at night so that the kids who miss you dearly can be compensated with a private education that could one day get them a great job with ridiculously long hours just like yours?

○ Couldn't you forgo the luxury holiday or expensive new bathroom for a day or a week of 'you time' and freedom?

○ Wouldn't it even be worth living on half your salary if it meant you felt relaxed, fulfilled and totally happy as a human being?

When I left my job five years ago to become a freelance writer, I did so because I felt that my life was being eaten away by work and I wanted more time to do the things that really made me feel like I was living. I knew that it would mean less money but I was more than happy to trade that in for more time. I wanted to be able to walk along the canal path near our home instead of being chained to my desk like a prisoner. I wanted the flexibility to choose how many hours I worked, and get paid for the work I had done, not the hours I had put in in captivity.

There are numerous options open to you if you want to free up some of your own life for yourself. You can work part-time, flexitime or consider a job share. You can start up your own consultancy or business, go freelance or do teleworking. Or you could just change your job for one that doesn't expect you to work such ridiculously long hours.

(340) FANCY WORKING JUST FOUR DAYS A WEEK?

9 to 5, Monday to Friday, right? Yes, it is the standard working week, but you'd be surprised how many employers might be open to the suggestion of allowing you to work less. You may even be in a role where they'd welcome the idea of reducing your hours.

(341) THE NEW TREND OF 'SUNLIGHTING'

A lot of people have dreams of other jobs that they would prefer to be doing. An accountant sits in his office dreaming of one day opening his own Italian delicatessen. A marketing exec working on the 24th floor of an office block would rather be growing rare orchids in a sun-filled greenhouse. A doctor wishes he had time to compose music for films and television.

'Sunlighting', as career specialists are now calling it, is a rapidly growing trend in which people work part-time in their first job and then use the extra days to take on a second job or pursue a freelance career. For example, one woman I spoke to recently has gone part time in her job as an events organiser and is launching herself in a career as an aromatherapist on the other days.

By persuading your employer to let you do a four-day week, you can free up one day a week which becomes absolutely YOURS. You get to pursue the things that you believe will make you really feel like you – but you have the security of money still coming in to pay the bills. If you're lucky and your extra job really takes off, that could even one day become your full-time job.

12) REMEMBER THAT LOOKING FOR A NEW JOB – OR WAY OF WORKING – CAN TAKE A REALLY LONG TIME

I have been rereading the classic and bestselling-ever career book, 'What Colour is Your Parachute?' by Richard Bolles. If you're even slightly thinking of changing your job or currently looking for a new one, then you really should read this book. It is full of advice that will not only make you much more successful in your job hunt, but also so much more happy and at ease in it as well.

Anyway . . . there are two pieces of advice that I particularly like from this very big and useful book:

1. You must be mentally prepared (and financially prepared) for your job hunt to last a lot longer than you think it will. Experienced outplacement people have long claimed that your search for one of the jobs that are out there will probably take one month for every £5,000 of salary that you are seeking. This may be pure drivel, but you get the picture, don't you?

2. The least effective method you may use for job hunting is looking through job ads. The most effective methods, in ascending order are: i) Ask family members and friends if they know of any jobs. ii) Knock on the door of any employer that interests you. iii) Use the Yellow Pages to look for jobs or employers that interest you then phone them. iv) Do number three with someone else or a group of people. v) Be creative about the way you look for work. Seek out the person who actually has the power to hire you for the job you want.

343) EARN TOO MUCH? WORK TOO MUCH? SPEND TOO MUCH?

You know who you are. All you have to do now is work out how to stop it. Wouldn't you prefer to just sit down quietly for a while and do nothing? Wouldn't it be nicer if it would all just STOP?

344) UNDERSTANDING YOUR LEGAL RIGHT TO FLEXITIME

Man or woman, if you have a child under six, you have the right to request flexible working hours from your employer. This does not mean that you have an automatic right to change your working hours but that your employer must seriously consider a request for flexible working arrangement and make efforts to make it possible.

345) DISCOVER THE JOYS OF JOB-SHARING

More and more people are now embracing the work–life balance revolution – and it's not just for women. A job-share is where one full-time job is split between two people. There is now an amazing 1% of employees who work on this basis, even at executive level. The Cabinet Office itself currently employs 12 members of staff on a job-share contract, and major companies that are offering it include Asda, HSBC, KPMG, the BBC and PricewaterhouseCoopers.

Could it be possible for you?

You don't know unless you ask. There is now a not inconsiderable number of job-share positions being advertised, particularly in public sector positions. What's more, as research now shows that job-sharers almost always out perform their full-time colleagues in terms of output, this certainly looks like a trend that's set to grow.

6) TO GET PROMOTED, STOP WORKING SO HARD

If you've ever felt like you're the only person in your company who actually works hard or cares about the work they do, read the book 'Hello Laziness: Why Hard Work Doesn't Pay' by Corinne Maier. It could well be that you're stressing too much and working a lot harder than you need to. In fact, you could actually be far more successful and happier in your job if you stop caring or working so hard!

7) TRADE YOUR JOB IN FOR 10 JOBS!

Bored of doing the same thing every day? Fed up with your boss or employer? Don't let fear of job insecurity chain you to the workplace. If you're the kind of person who's prepared to work, there will always be as much (or as little) well-paid work out there for you as you can handle. All it takes is a bit of searching, perseverance, nerve and ingenuity. Take gutter clearing, for example. It might not be very glamorous but you don't need any formal qualifications for doing it and you can earn about £70 or £80 a time. Or how about research? Earning £10 or £20 an hour may not add up to the most amazing salary, but if you're the kind of person who relishes the idea of spending all day in a library then this could be your dream occupation. You may even end up working for a famous novelist or for a TV programme!

Quitting your job can be terrifying, so it may be worth starting to build up at least some 'portfolio jobs' in your spare time before you finally pull the plug.

Other jobs you could use to create a 'portfolio' of work include:

- eBay trading
- Writing articles
- Gardening
- House-sitting
- Product demonstrating
- CV writing
- Importing furniture or jewellery
- Proof reading
- Desktop publishing
- Mystery shopping
- Bar work
- Making cakes for dogs' birthdays ...

348) WORK LESS TO EARN MORE

Many of us are driven by a work ethic that makes us believe that we need to work more and harder if we want to earn more. If you really want to earn more, however, it may actually pay you to look for ways to earn significant amounts of money while actually working less. If you are paid by the hour – particularly if it's at a low rate – then you're never going to earn that much.

349) WORK FOR YOURSELF OR START YOUR OWN BUSINESS

It will only happen if you take very big and brave steps to make it do so. The best way to start is to begin gathering as much information and advice as possible. Search on the Web. Buy books on the subject. Make arrangements to sit down and talk to people who've done something similar to what you'd like to do.

350) START YOUR OWN BUSINESS – WITH FREE MONEY

The total value of grants and support schemes available to businesses in the UK is estimated at some £5 billion per annum. A lot of that money, however, is not getting claimed because people are not aware that these schemes exist. Another option for funding is to find a business angel. Business angels are wealthy individuals who will put money (and often time and expertise) into your business in return for a share of equity. The National Business Angels Network (NBAN) estimates that there are currently 18,000 Business Angels in the UK investing roughly £500 million into 3,500 businesses every year.

The best way to find out about both grants available and business angels is through the Enterprise Advisory Service. A one-off subscription of £49.50 for a year gets you access to information on over 3,000 grant schemes currently open to UK applicants. It also gives you access to information on sources of Venture Capital and Business Angels. Visit their website at www.govgrantsglobal.com, or write to Enterprise Advisory Service International, 4 Sussex Road, Southsea, Portsmouth, Hampshire PO5 3EX.

(351) WORK LOCALLY

Fancy a new job or career but don't know where to start? Fed up with the commute and the way that doing your job eats up 90% of your day? One interesting method for picking a new job, forcing a change or opening up new options is to look for something that would only be a 5–20 minute commute (and preferably walk) from your home. If you like the idea of getting calmly home at 5.30 PM instead of stressfully home by 7.30 PM, you could find out, for example, if there are any companies in your area who could be looking for people with your skills. This could be a far better option than commuting into London or doing the 40-minute drive you are at the moment. You may even find that changing your job brings you in a higher salary. In fact, most people who change their job within their profession will be able to obtain a higher salary by doing so.

Or maybe working locally could mean a complete career and lifestyle change. Working as a librarian, school teacher, carpenter, counsellor, tree surgeon or milkman could actually be the lifestyle change you're looking for.

52) DO YOU REALLY HATE YOUR JOB THAT MUCH?

Moaning about your job is standard practice – a bit like British people talking about the weather. Yet for many people, when it really comes down to it, their job is actually a major source of happiness. Work is the place where you get to do something really well and be proud of the talent you have. Work is where you meet with other people and share in a community spirit.

I met someone once whose friend had won the lottery. They still worked every day as a JCB driver because they absolutely loved it. What would life be without a digger to drive, mates to chat to and a jumbo sausage roll for lunch?

53) MAKE MORE OF YOUR LUNCH BREAK

If you can't change your work, then why not change the way you work? For starters, you must make sure you take advantage of your lunch break. You have a statutory right to a break from your work and a moral right to do something better with it than stuff your face with a sandwich while mindlessly sitting at your computer trawling the internet.

Why not see if there are any lunchtime concerts or exhibitions you can go to? Many universities and colleges offer lunchtime lectures. Or, with 240 hours of lunch breaks a year, you could even use the time to study for an Open University Degree.

If you want to slow down your life, then why not spend the time practising meditation or attending a yoga class. Or, if you're still keen to fit more into your life in less time, opt for a rock climbing session, join a lunch dating agency (www.rapidromance .com, www.onlylunch.co.uk) or do a weekly volunteering

session at a local elderly day care centre or hospital (www.csv
.org.uk).

354. WHY YOU DESERVE TO EARN TWICE AS MUCH AS YOU DO TODAY

You're a very talented person and you earn a decent wage. But
do you know what? You actually deserve to earn a lot more.

Artistically minded people in particular are often prone to
feel that they don't really deserve to earn a lot of money. It is
likely to come across to them as a feeling that they do not wish
to earn that much – or that it is a dirty or unethical thing to do
so. Realise that you deserve to be really well remunerated for
your talent. Money is *not* a dirty thing and flows very freely. It
is what you do with it that is important.

21

MOVING OVERSEAS

○ How you really could start a new life in Canada, Australia or even the sunny coast of Mexico
○ Smart ways of finding a job overseas
○ A beautiful new home for just £50,000

Fed up with the high cost of living in the UK? Bored with the weather, the culture, the politics or the people? Ever fancied moving to a cheaper, sunnier and nicer country? Somewhere you could work less, live more and stop feeling so stressed and exhausted all the time? Somewhere where people are really positive about life and you have stunning scenery on your doorstep?

Then why not just do it?

As Britain is currently one of the most expensive countries in the world in which to live, making a move overseas makes very good sense as a 'Spend Less, Live Better' policy. It could be much easier to pull off than you might imagine. And it could actually be the most wonderful, life-affirming and life-transforming move you ever make.

Why commute through the grey rain five days a week to live in a country where the cost of housing and living is so high that most of your hard-earned wages go on just paying for the basics?

Most of us have had moments on holiday when we've seriously wondered whether we couldn't actually live somewhere truly beautiful and amazing. So what's stopping you from actually doing it?

> Why not move somewhere where the sun always shines, the air is clean and you can buy a bottle of good wine for £1.50?

The following tips are not meant as a comprehensive guide to relocating overseas, but rather as some inspiration to help you realise that you really could turn those dreams into reality.

(355) AUSTRALIA IS LOOKING FOR QUALIFIED PROFESSIONALS JUST LIKE YOU

Australia is one of the most popular emigration destinations in the world. It offers a high standard of living, a great climate, more space and beauty than you could imagine and a smile on your face all year round.

If you've ever wondered who can apply for migration to Australia then here's a list of just some of the professions and skilled workers who are welcome to apply (as long as they have relevant qualifications and work experience):

Architects, accountants, chemists, meteorologists, surveyors, material scientists, engineers, marketing and sales professionals, IT professionals (such as systems programmers and software designers), statisticians, nurses, midwives, dentists, pharmacists, occupational therapists, chiropractors, osteopaths, vets, acupuncturists, doctors, primary and secondary school teachers, dance teachers, social workers, solicitors, journalists, editors, graphic designers, jewellers, dress makers, senior managers, piano tuners, picture framers, watch and clock makers, locksmiths, gunsmiths, welders, blacksmiths, motor mechanics, butchers, bakers, cooks, electricians, carpenters, nursery persons, plumbers, bricklayers, roof slaters and panel beaters.

Making a change in your life can be an incredibly hard thing to do. The only way to start is to get the ball rolling. You could start by getting a free assessment of your chances of getting a work or business visa from internet sites like www.thinking-australia.com or www.migrationexpert.com.

356) *SEARCH FOR INTERNATIONAL JOBS IN YOUR FIELD*

Get on the web and start looking for jobs in your area of expertise.

- Try the portal www.transitionsabroad.com for a whole list of websites where you can search for jobs by profession or country.
- Ask at your current company if there are ever opportunities to work overseas.
- Do clever internet searches to discover how you can find out about job availabilities in the countries you'd like to live in. What would be the equivalent of *The Guardian* job pages in Australia, for example? Which are the big accountancy

or publishing firms in Canada and why not contact them directly? Contact friends of friends who already live there and ask them to send you information on local job hunting.

(357) *CONSIDER A CHANGE OF CAREER?*

With certain professions, goods and services highly in demand in other countries, a move overseas could even be the answer to your career dilemmas as well. Retrain as an osteopath and get a job in Australia? Sell up your home and open an international food shop or interior design shop in Budapest? Use the cheaper housing and living costs of Portugal to relocate and start a career in writing, dog breeding or international importing and exporting?

(358) *CANADA ACTIVELY SEEKING SKILLED WORKERS*

Due to growth in the Canadian economy and a continued shortage of skilled workers, the Canadian government is very keen to attract skilled workers to live and work in Canada. With approximately 150,000 work rights visas available for economic class applicants every year, why shouldn't you be one of them? If you are well educated, have good work experience in your expertise or are keen to start a new business, you stand a good chance of getting a visa. You can get a free assessment at websites like www.migrationexpert.com.

(359) *YOU HAVE THE RIGHT TO APPLY FOR ANY JOB IN THE EU*

As a member of the EU, you have the automatic right to apply for – and of course take – any job advertised in the EU. An employer may obviously decide to turn down your application if you do not speak the local language, but then speaking English in some jobs may actually be an advantage.

You can turn up at the local job centre in any EU town and apply for the jobs they have advertised there. You can apply for jobs in papers or with job agencies. And of course, in areas where a lot of expat Brits are already living, there may even be the possibility of being employed by a British-owned shop, business or company based overseas.

YOU ALSO HAVE THE RIGHT TO 'SIGN ON' IN ANY COUNTRY IN THE EU WHILE YOU LOOK FOR WORK

You are not entitled to unemployment benefit in another EU country unless you have worked there. You are, however, entitled to claim UK Jobseeker's Allowance while looking for work anywhere in the EU. You need to have been registered unemployed for at least four weeks in the UK and can then arrange to have the allowance paid to you while living in another country for up to three months. This is fantastic for anyone who wants to start a new life overseas but is worried about financial insecurity if they can't find work when they get there. Make sure you inform Jobcentre Plus of your intention to look for work elsewhere, usually at least six weeks before your departure.

HOW ANYONE CAN WORK THEIR WAY AROUND THE WORLD

Fancy working at a horse trekking centre in Iceland? At turtle conservation in Costa Rica? Teaching English in Moscow? Football in New England? Or being a ski bum in Val d'Iser?

If you haven't got kids to worry about (and even if you have), there's no reason why you can't spend the rest of your life (or just six months or a year of it) drifting around the world, picking up jobs and living the sweet life of Riley. If you have a mortgage in the UK, you can rent your home out while you're away and stay on the good old property ladder while having more fun in a few months than most of your friends will have in their lifetime. This could also be an ideal way to try and 'sort your head out'.

The best source of information is a great book called 'Work Your Way Around the World' by Susan Griffith. For example, she tells us that in France 100,000 foreign workers are employed on the grape harvest alone.

"It is possible to support yourself throughout the year in France by combining work in the various fruit harvests with either conventional jobs such as tutoring in English, or more unusual occupations from busking to gathering snails."

A good website to try is www.paris-anglo.com.

There is a story about a woman who saved £3,000 in five months working as a chef in Gibraltar. If you went out to Spanish countries like Ibiza, Tenerife or Lanzarote, you'd almost certainly be able to find work there. In the Czech Republic there is plenty of work available for English teachers (try www.akcent.cz, for example). And remember that in a lot of temporary work situations, you will find that accommodation is provided for you.

Further afield, you might try teaching English at one of the 30 language schools in Santiago, Chile. In Australia you could pick lemons from July to October, get a job as a truck driver or become an au pair or a nanny. For English teaching jobs in Thailand try the website www.ajarn.com.

2) TAKE ADVANTAGE OF LOWER PROPERTY AND LIVING COSTS TO SET UP A BUSINESS IN THE EU

As an EU resident you have the same rights to start up your own business as you do here in the UK. Sell up your expensive home in the UK and you might find you have enough money to start a new life abroad doing the work you want to do.

3) IT IS STILL POSSIBLE TO PICK UP A COTTAGE IN FRANCE FOR AS LITTLE AS €45,000

Avoid the popular areas of the Dordogne and Provence and you can still find affordable French properties in beautiful unspoilt towns – as yet virtually undiscovered by hordes of other English! The Chalosse and the Pays de l'Adour, for example, have beautiful and peaceful countrysides and are now much more accessible – thanks to Ryanair flights to Pau. If you find yourself getting serious about the move, you might consider employing a personal property searcher from the Granny Network (www.grannynetwork.info). For €300, they will personally search the area for suitable properties on your behalf, send you photos, arrange your viewings and will even help out with the transactions.

LOOK FURTHER AFIELD FOR CHEAPER PROPERTY

Sixty thousand Brits bought property in Spain in 2004 and this is still one of the most favoured destinations. If you fancy something a bit cheaper and less popular, however, there are plenty of other countries to consider. Cyprus, for example, has good weather all year, almost no crime, and English is spoken everywhere as the second language. You could easily pick up a very nice apartment for around £70,000 – 100,000, mortgages are available for foreigners and – unlike Spain – this is still a very new market for overseas buyers.

 NEVER STOP DREAMING. HOW ABOUT A PARADISE BEACH HOUSE?

Americans aren't always right, but they know a good thing when they see it. Right now, they're snapping up cheap property in fantastic destinations like Mexico, Argentina, Nicaragua, the Dominican Republic and Ecuador. If you cashed out of your mortgage with say £100,000 today, you'd have enough money to buy a beautiful property in one of these countries outright. Maybe even two. With no rent or mortgage to pay and the cost of living low, what couldn't you do with your life and the beach just round the corner?

I can see it now. . . .

CONCLUSION

"Money isn't everything; usually it isn't even enough."

Anon

I thought I would end with a quote that was at least a little contradictory to the somewhat sanctimonious quotation that I started with in the introduction.

You see, while it's important to realise that money isn't everything, it's also important not to force yourself to go too much the other way.

You shouldn't beat yourself up if you find yourself staring in a shop window at a beautiful suit or pair of £250 shoes. And yes, bluebells in a jam jar are lovely but, hell, why not blow £30 now and again on a big bouquet that comes with all that cellophane and ribbon and a feeling that you've really got somewhere in life?

A certain amount of extravagance and waste is essential for our sanity. Indeed, many societies have festivals dedicated to just that. For Christians it has traditionally been Christmas. During the Middle Ages and the Renaissance, the year was punctuated by a series of feasts. Even very primitive societies have festivals where they set fire to canoes.

Remember, materialism and capitalism are not actually bad in themselves. What is wrong with wanting a comfy sofa to sit on, clothes that make you feel good, or a TV that enables you to be inspired by snow leopards or uplifted by your favourite comedy? And what is wrong with a society and a system that enables everybody within it to have those things?

The bad only comes when things get out of hand or when they start diminishing rather than improving the quality of your life.

Money is something that most of us simply assume that we haven't got enough of. And that, in fact, is where a lot of the harm begins.

Above all, I hope this book has helped you stop money issues from ruining your life – and to make sure every penny is working towards making your life better. I hope it has done something to help you make the money that you have go further. And I hope it will help you get more of the things that you really want out of life.

ABOUT THE AUTHOR

Rebecca Ash studied philosophy, French and psychology, then spent the first years of her working life in China living on £80 a month. She moved back to London where she became a copywriter and spent the next ten years trying to persuade other people to buy, buy, buy . . . spend, spend, spend – and herself that she liked it. Rebecca has now quit that job, quit London and quit spending, and is a freelance writer who is raising her two children away from the city.

BB	2|09
BL	